GAZ

THE AUTOBIOGRAPHY OF
A LEAGUE LEGEND

GAZ
MARK GASNIER

AND ANDREW WEBSTER

EBURY
PRESS

An Ebury Press book
Published by Random House Australia Pty Ltd
Level 3, 100 Pacific Highway, North Sydney NSW 2060
www.randomhouse.com.au

First published by Ebury Press in 2012

Addresses for companies within the Random House Group can be found at www.randomhouse.com.au/offices

National Library of Australia
Cataloguing-in-Publication Entry

Gasnier, Mark.
Gaz / Mark Gasnier.

ISBN 9781742755274 (pbk.)

Gasnier, Mark.
Rugby League football players – Australia – Biography.
Rugby League football – Australia – Biography.
Rugby League football – Australia – Anecdotes.
Rugby Union football – France.

796.3338092

Cover design by Blue Cork
Cover portrait by fa tog'ra fi
Internal design by Post Pre-press Group
Typeset in 12.5/17 pt Minion Regular by Post Pre-press Group
Printed in Australia by Griffin Press, an accredited ISO AS/NZS 14001:2004 Environmental Management System printer

Random House Australia uses papers that are natural, renewable and recyclable products and made from wood grown in sustainable forests. The logging and manufacturing processes are expected to conform to the environmental regulations of the country of origin.

A lot was written and said throughout my career.
What follows is my version of everything that took place.

CONTENTS

FOREWORD

By NATHAN BROWN

IT WAS ABOUT 2004 when I sat Mark Gasnier down and told him how I saw it. The conversation went something like this:

'Your life's marked out, mate. We can all see it. Your uncle was the game's greatest ever centre. How often, in any sport, does lightning strike twice? How often does the next greatest centre of his generation come from the same family, play for the same club, have the ability to do the same things? It doesn't seem real.

'Gaz, you can play State of Origins and Test matches. You'll probably win a Grand Final, too. And then you'll get a job in the media – you'll be set up for the rest of your life. You can live and surf and enjoy your life with no pressure. Most people's lives are never that simple. You're a good style of bloke, but the only person who can bring that tumbling down is you.'

I laid out that path for Gaz in my second year of coaching the Dragons; he was my right centre. But, like everything in life, it would never be that simple.

Let me go back to the start.

The first Gasnier I ever saw was a prop. He was a skilful front-runner and a smart footballer. Gavin Gasnier was the eldest of John and Janene's four boys, and he was my St George teammate playing under-17s in the early 1990s.

Gav was a good footballer, and a great bloke, but by then everyone in the club was talking about his youngest brother. Everyone knew of Reg Gasnier, the Immortal centre who was an icon of the club and the game of rugby league. But everyone was *talking* about Reg's nephew, and everyone knew he was really good.

Mark Gasnier was just 10 years old.

I played with him in his debut match, when he had been called up at the last minute against the Knights after Matt Cooper had suffered an injury in the warm-up. Gaz was this big, rangy athlete, but you knew straightaway that he was foremost a footballer. He came on the scene at a time when rugby league players were becoming more athlete than footballer. Mark was an athlete but he also had wonderful hands, a killer sidestep, and above all he knew how to position his winger. Not everyone who comes into rugby league knows how to play the game. They don't know what is required to play the game like a classic centre. Gaz already knew.

The interesting thing is that he never chose to be this way. For a lot of kids who play rugby league, it's their number one love. Gaz's first love was surfing. If not for the surname, he'd have had a surfboard under his arm and would've been more comfortable in life. Instead, he went down the path that life chose for him, because of where he came from and the simple fact that he was an outstanding talent.

That famous surname was always there, of course. It never bothered Gaz. He respected what his Uncle Reg had done, but it was his father, John, who had been the real influence on his life. John Gasnier is such a good person, and was such a good father, but whenever Mark's name popped up in the media during the early years of his career, it was Reg's name that was mentioned. Alongside Janene and his brothers, John helped create a son and a brother to be proud of.

In my opinion, the greatest thing that ever happened to Mark Gasnier was probably the most embarrassing: his infamous voicemail message on the eve of his State of Origin debut in 2004. I know Gaz as well as anyone. I played with him. I coached him. I've seen him grow as a person, as I've grown as a person.

Because of that incident, Mark changed. He was always a good man, but being held accountable helped him grow up. Before, if he ever did something wrong nothing happened, as is the case with so many sportsmen around the world today – rugby league, cricket, whatever. They get older and still expect the whole world to give them something. They're rarely held responsible. But Gaz was. He was held accountable by that error of judgement, and it has helped him grow into a good teammate, a good husband, a good father. It was the making of him.

He needed to have a strong character because our years

together at the Dragons were tough times. I always had the greatest confidence in his ability. If you've got someone of Gaz's talent on your team, you've got to use it. You want to get the best out of him. I wanted as many game plans as possible to work around Gaz, but in hindsight I think I could've used him better.

Players of Mark's calibre can play anywhere. He would've made it at full-back for sure. Whether he was going to be a great five-eighth was debatable, but that's where we were going to play him for the 2007 season, after our captain, Trent Barrett, had been squeezed out because of the inevitable salary cap pressure that bites every club.

I felt that 2007 season was going to be his best year. It was the hungriest I'd ever seen him, and he'd trained the house down that pre-season. Then he tore his pectoral muscle in the Charity Shield against South Sydney – another bad injury for Gaz, who had seen too many throughout his career already. If not for injury, who knows just how good Mark Gasnier could've been?

But there were other things he had to deal with. We all did.

I started coaching the Dragons when I was 28 – still a young bloke by anyone's standards. I had only just become a husband and was still some way off becoming a father. I was mates with a lot of the players, because I had played with them. It's not like the coach can't be friends with his team, but you need rapport to build over time. It was a tough situation that I would never advise any coach to enter into.

For all the glory and pride of being involved with any

great club, nobody will understand the pressure of coaching the famous Red V. Admittedly, some teams have been around for longer. South Sydney has won more premierships. The Broncos are an outstanding club that many reckon are the benchmark. But nothing will ever outshine the Dragons, because of their history. No other sporting side in the world has won 11 premierships in a row. No league team produced three of the first four Immortals. Those feats will never be repeated. The legend of Reg and Chook and Chang and Billy Smith will always be there, and the more Grand Finals we lost and the more times that we fell short, the more the pressure grew on us all.

And that's when the rubbish started. It seemed to be mainly directed at four people: Trent Barrett, Peter Doust, myself . . . and Gaz. Trent was in the crosshairs because he was a high-profile player, well recognised and our captain; Dousty, the chief executive, was the one who stood by us; I was coach and their mate; and Gaz had the surname.

It was a tough time for a lot of people involved, for different reasons, and until that premiership drought was broken, the pressure was always going to be there. Some of us had to leave for it to go away. Trent went to play in Wigan; I went to Huddersfield to coach; and Gaz was forced out of the club because of contract issues and went to Paris to play rugby union. He had to leave because of financial issues – nobody begrudged him going – but in some ways it helped him grow, just like the Origin incident.

When Wayne Bennett joined the club as my replacement in 2009, some of the pressure was released for the players still there. When they won the premiership in 2010, I remember telling someone that the victory had set free many of us who had been there for the past 30 years. You could look back and think 'if only' you had been involved in the achievement in some way. I played in three losing Grand Finals and coached in that period when we had a good roster but couldn't go the distance.

When they finally won, it was a relief. The next one we'll probably enjoy more.

I'm just glad Gaz was able to come back from Paris and be a part of it. He deserved it as much as any of us. As I said to him all those years ago, maybe it was already marked out for him. A Gasnier to make his mark, in his own right.

ONE

TO PARIS WITH LOVE

FOR AS LONG AS I can remember, I had no control over it.

All I knew was that it felt right, even if it didn't always come off as I'd planned. I can't explain it. It just happened. I am out here on the right side of the field, the green turf of Kogarah Oval beneath my feet, and I am set deep. I am standing in the centres and Trent Barrett is drifting my way. He is our five-eighth, our playmaker, and he reels off one of those perfect, left-to-right spiral passes of his. It fizzes through the air and the white Steeden thuds into my chest, right on the Red V emblazoned across my white jersey.

I'm looking directly at my opposite centre's feet. I wait. I'm waiting for the instant when his feet are planted to the ground – *both* of them. Once he does that, I'm certain I've got him done. You can call it arrogance or self-belief – and I would never say it came *easy* – but it is what it is.

That's when it happens. The part I have no control over. I don't know if I'm going left or going right. My head never tells my sidestep what to do. It just happens. I've got no control over it.

Whatever you do, don't call it a 'shimmy'. And it's not a 'shimmy-shimmy-*whoosh!*' as Phil Gould would call in his commentary on Channel Nine – something my teammates revelled in sledging me about for many years.

But in 174 games of first grade for St George Illawarra, in 12 State of Origins for NSW and 15 Test matches for my country, and even before any of that, the split decision meant everything to me.

Unfortunately, footy is never just about one frozen moment on the field. It's the stuff on the other side of the sideline that is just as hard to control. And it was that part of the game that threatened everything . . .

It is two days before game two of the 2008 State of Origin series, and I am about to walk away from rugby league. And, in my mind, walk away forever.

Two years earlier I'd signed a new deal that tied me to the Dragons – and the game – for five years. The deal was worth $660,000 a season, with $310,000 of that made up in agreements with four other sponsors.

As I started the 2008 season, I'd kept up my end of the bargain. I'd done all the work required – but not one of the sponsors had paid me. Nothing. Not a cent.

It starts to build. Each time I step on the field there is a knot in my stomach, and it's becoming tighter and tighter with every month.

That split second that always came easily does not come so easily anymore. My form starts to mirror exactly how I am feeling off the field. I am losing weight through the financial stress of knowing that almost half my wage isn't being paid – if it will ever be paid at all. I start getting a nervous rash on my body. It's shingles. It recurs three times. Sometimes I play well, but deep down I know I can't play consistent footy because I'm in a bad place.

Yes, I'm on a good wage, but I know the value of hard work. Nothing was ever handed to me. I come from a working-class family, having grown up in Mortdale in the south of Sydney, right in the heart of St George territory. And I have mortgages, investments and commitments like everyone else, all of it budgeted on the amount of money I earn.

I've had enough. I phone my manager, George Mimis. 'George,' I say, 'I can't keep going. Something has to give. I'm not crying poor, but I'll have to sell something. I need to know where I'm heading.'

So I set a deadline of 1 June. If the money isn't paid – even if *some* of the money isn't paid – something will have to give.

The deadline comes and passes. Now it is 9 June. In two days it will be State of Origin II, when I will run out into the middle of a heaving Suncorp Stadium in Brisbane wearing a sky-blue jumper, hoping to help New South Wales to its first series win in two years.

But my mind is elsewhere. I am in knots again. Every spare minute is sucked up talking on the phone. I call George: 'I can't stay. What would you do? I've got to go.'

We've been speaking to French rugby clubs. I don't want to go to another code, or another country, but I have no alternative. For weeks now most of the dialogue has been with Biarritz, a famous club in the south of France, but then Ewen McKenzie calls.

He's still coaching the NSW Waratahs, but he'd been told earlier this year that he wasn't required after this Super Rugby season. He's just signed with Stade Francais, the glamour club that plays out of Paris. He has a question to ask me: do I want to come, too?

I'm in a Brisbane hotel room. The knots tighten again, constricting like never before . . . There is nothing I can do. I agree to terms to join Stade Francais as soon as my contract with the Dragons expires.

At the start of this year, I had been named captain of the Dragons. It was the proudest moment of my career. I had never showed how much it meant to me. Now I am numb.

So here's game night. Suncorp erupts with Maroon pride, like it always does. I'd played very well up against Greg Inglis in our victory over Queensland in the first game of the series in Sydney – something that's not easily done because he's one of the best centres in the world.

Not this time. With my football fate sealed and my head all over the place, Inglis runs around me like I'm not even there. He sets up Darius Boyd for two tries and Queensland rolls on to win 30–0, keeping the series alive. They will eventually go on and win the whole thing.

I'm embarrassed and pissed off and almost ashamed, because I am better than that. And while I know the reason why I have just produced quite possibly the worst game of my career, I know I can't say it out loud.

First, because the whole thing with French rugby is confidential. I've agreed to terms, but I haven't signed anything. I haven't told a soul outside of my family about what is happening. But more than that, I don't want to make excuses. To do that would make me look like a sook, and that's not what I'm about.

Two days later, I am downstairs in George's office in Sydney. That office: I've spent countless hours there in the last few months, trying to work out where my mixed-up career is going, trying to straighten it out. It is nearly 10 pm when the official contract from Stade Francais comes through on the fax machine. I sign the documents, we fax them back, and that's it: the deal is done.

The first bloke I phone is Peter Doust, the Dragons chief executive who did everything he could to stop this from happening. This is the hardest call I'll ever make.

'Gaz, I know the situation,' he says to me. 'I just don't want you to have any regrets. I don't want you to throw away what you've worked so hard to achieve in the game. We can have it resolved.'

I've always loved Dousty's optimism. He's a father of four and knows how the game and the Dragons work as much as anyone. 'I can't hold on any longer, mate,' I tell him. 'Because if I do, and it doesn't work out, I'll be in a bigger hole.'

Then the whole thing becomes public, and the shit hits the fan.

The accusations come from everywhere, most of them directed at me. Sonny Bill Williams had left the game earlier this year to play French rugby. Now me. Traitor. Disloyal. Mercenary. Money hungry.

Some say I had pushed other players out of the club because of the salary cap, and now I am abandoning them. Steve Morris, a former Dragon, fingers me for pushing his son Josh out and to the Bulldogs. Gorden Tallis, another former Dragon, says I should never be allowed to come back. Ricky Stuart, who had been my coach for NSW and Australia and a good mate, won't return my calls.

Thankfully, my coach, Nathan Brown, and my teammates know the score. I'd kept them abreast of what was going on every step of the way. They'd seen the frustration boiling inside of me. They know I wanted to stay.

The only upshot is that at least I know what I'm doing. We settle down and play enough respectable footy to finish in seventh position and qualify for the play-offs.

Then we play our first final against Manly at Brookvale Oval and they smack us 38–6. Sitting in the steamy away dressing-room, no one barely says a word to each other. It's understandable. It's the end of an era. Browny is leaving the club. So is prop Jason Ryles, my closest mate in the team. I'm looking forward to getting back to St George Leagues Club and having a few beers with my teammates – my mates – because I don't know when I'll get the next chance.

On the way there, though, my mobile rings. Another phone call. Stade Francais has booked me on an early-morning flight from Sydney to Paris. As in tomorrow morning. They want me there as soon as possible.

So I have two beers, say goodbye, and walk out of the club that had been my life for as long as I could remember. I have never wanted to play for any other club, and now I'm turning my back on it. The knots tighten again.

And as I leave that night, heading to a new country, a new club, a new code and a new life, I am angry. Filthy. But maybe of greater concern is the fact that I am certain I will never come back to rugby league again. It's over.

No player has a perfect ride throughout his entire career. If he tells you it's all been paved with gold, he's a liar. But I guess I had as many highs and lows than anyone, if not more.

The most important part is what shape you're in when you come out the other side. About how it ends. This is how I got there.

TWO

MOO

I'VE BEEN CALLED PLENTY of things over the years, but most people in rugby league know me as 'Gaz'. But for as long as I can remember, from the earliest age, the people closest to me have called me 'Moo'.

My father, John, had a milk run, and we always had a Moove in our hands. Dad would call me 'Moo Juicer' or 'Marky Moo'. My three elder brothers still call me 'Moo'. Even my nephew calls me 'Uncle Moo'. Right up until my final game of footy, if I ran onto the field and heard someone say, 'C'mon, Mooey!' I knew straightaway that it was one of the boys I'd grown up with.

As for Mum, well, she usually just calls me Mark.

It wasn't until I was twelve that I realised the significance of my surname. Kids in the schoolyard at Oatley West Public would ask me if I could get old Reg Gasnier footy cards signed for them. Well, not for them, but their parents. After a while, I asked Mum and Dad what it was all about. 'Did Uncle Reg play football?'

That's when Dad explained everything to me, pulling out some old VHS tapes that showed Reg in black and white and in full flight from the 1960s, when the Dragons were just about unbeatable on their way to their fabled eleven consecutive premierships.

What did I think? He was a freak. His change of pace, his ability to get around defenders, his instinct on the footy field in general. As we were watching them, Dad explained that while Reg wasn't known for his toughness, he actually was. He played with plenty of bumps and bruises.

It probably doesn't fit with the script some might like, but that wasn't the moment when a shaft of light came down from above and I said out loud: 'Footy – that's what I want to do!'

Until that point, I had no clue about the standing Uncle Reg had in football and Australian sport in general. I didn't know he was one of the best centres – if not *the* best – to have played the game. I didn't know about the bloke who had played nine seasons for St George, who had been affectionately known as 'Puff the Magic Dragon', who had dazzled the crowds from Kogarah to the Sydney Cricket Ground to the famous grounds in England and France while playing for the Kangaroos.

To me, he was just Uncle Reg, the bloke I saw at barbecues and family christenings and on Christmas Day. I mean, how often do you see your own uncle?

Nothing was ever made in our house about the legend

surrounding our last name, and that's because of the down-to-earth type of family we were – and still are.

★

I was born in St Vincent's Hospital, in the Sydney suburb of Paddington, on 19 July 1981, and I was the fourth and last of four boys for John and Janene Gasnier. I'm pretty sure I was a pleasant surprise, because they'd already had three boys: Gavin, who is the oldest and six years older than me; Brent, five years older; and Dean, four years older.

Shortly after I was born the family moved to Tamworth, but two years later we were back in Sydney, moving into Balmoral Road in Mortdale Heights, right in the heart of St George territory.

This might surprise some people, but there's actually more football and Red V tradition on Mum's side of the family. Her father, Stan Lapham, played first grade for St George and his brother Trevor played lower grades for the club. Dad reckoned Trevor was one of the best players he'd seen, but the Dragons didn't want him because he had come on in his football at an older age.

It was Mum's uncle, Ernie, who was the real superstar. 'Curly' Lapham played with St George in their first game in the premiership in 1921, and was rated one of the best and fastest forwards in the game for his time. He could sniff out a try, too, and after joining Souths in 1925 was a crucial part in their four successive premierships. He went on and played for NSW.

Dad was a winger and played third grade for St George in 1969, when he was called up from playing A-grade with Renown United at the age of 28. That was the year the legendary Dragons five-eighth Brian 'Poppa' Clay was thirds coach, before he suffered a heart attack and Paul Broughton took over. I imagine it wouldn't have been easy following in the footsteps of Uncle Reg – who had retired two years earlier – and Dad retired after that.

So the game was in my blood. If I was a racehorse, I might have been worth a bit.

Ironically, while Mum and Dad loved the Red V, my brothers and I supported other teams. I loved the Raiders because of Laurie Daley and Ricky Stuart, and would wear Canberra jumpers, with the iconic Woodger's badge on the front and No.7 on the back, until they didn't fit me any longer. I remember seeing Canberra play St George at Kogarah Oval one day, and I couldn't believe the size of the players – they were huge!

Despite the pedigree, despite my early loyalties, rugby league wasn't my life. It wasn't even my first love. I had a taste of all sports growing up – cricket, Aussie rules, rugby – but it was surfing that I couldn't get enough of. Brent and his friends got their licences when I was about nine, and I'd go out with them all the time. When I got to the age when Mum let me catch the train, my mates and I would get the 4:49 am train to Cronulla before school, have a surf, then catch the 7:36 back in time for class. I subscribed to *Surfing Life*, and that was about the only thing I read.

I started playing rugby league when I was five years old,

but in the under-7s, for Renown United, the famous Mortdale club where Dad and Uncle Reg had played. It's the same club that produced the great Billy Smith and, in more recent times, Jason Nightingale.

When I was 13, I wore the Red V for the first time, playing in the Harold Matthews representative competition for under-15s. Col Tricker was the coach and a family friend, and because Mum and Dad were working so much, he would be the one who took me to and from training. He saw something in me, and I have always appreciated it.

The Harold Matthews competition goes for six weeks, and when that was over I would go up to the SG Ball competition (under-17s) instead of returning to play junior footy with Renown. I was a skinny kid but I was quick and could step, and it was after my second season of Harold Matthews that the player managers came sniffing around. The Dragons were really keen and wanted me to sign a seven-year deal with them.

That's when I was ready to turn my back on rugby league. I don't want to sound disrespectful – I loved the game – but I didn't know if I wanted it to be my life. By then, all my mates had quit footy so they could surf. I actually said to my parents, 'No, I want to quit. I don't want to do this.'

There are a couple of reasons, and I hope it shows in some ways the type of level-headed person I am and the people who shaped me.

While we never went without, it wasn't easy for my parents to make a life for their four boys. They worked several jobs each; Mum in a florist and a giftware shop, while Dad did shiftwork of a night and mowed lawns during the day. Dad is a workaholic – always has been. And he's the most placid bloke on the face of the planet. I've seen him angry only once: when a neighbour swore at Mum.

The best thing he ever did was making us work for our money. Nothing was ever given to us. We'd help him mow his lawns and he'd give us $50 to split for the day. He made all four of us buy our own cars – my first was a Datsun 180Y. It was as orange as a pumpkin.

Life with three older brothers was hilarious. We were constantly at each other. It was always Gav and me against Brent and Dean. Brent's nickname was 'Boozer', because as a baby he would grab at Dad's beer. Deano's nickname was 'Crusher', as in Noel 'Crusher' Cleal, because he was so big as a kid. The sledging between the four of us never ended, and Gav would often have to stick up for me. I was a real little smart-arse. Very cheeky.

The simplest things amused us. We were never inside, always together, usually on the golf course or the rubbish tip adjacent to our house. We'd find golf balls and sell them back to the members, or scavenge through the tip for things of value, and that gave us enough money to buy electrical tape for strapping when we played footy.

We didn't really have money to buy new clothes for school, so Mum would hand me down stuff from my brothers, sewing on the latest label from a hot surfwear brand. We would think it was a great new pair of shorts. We never knew any differently.

I used to get all their footy boots, too. It's amazing how much you appreciate football boots and things like that back then. When you come into first grade, you're truly grateful to be given whatever you want. Dad used to say you played better with polished boots, so I polished them up before every game.

As a student at Oatley West Public and then Peakhurst High, I had the attention span as big as a mouse. My three brothers never went past Year 10, and I was heading in the same direction. Every school report card was the same: 'If Mark paid attention, if he applied himself, he could do really well.' But, to be honest, by the time I reached Year 10 I knew I was either going to take up a trade like Dad and the boys, which I had no problems with whatsoever, or play footy. I knew you didn't have to learn life from a textbook. My parents and brothers taught me that.

While I was close to all of my brothers, Gav and I were the tightest. He was a very intelligent bloke and footballer. He was a prop with a lot of skill. He'd come through the grades with the likes of Gorden Tallis and Nathan Brown, and was on the bench for first grade when he was 17. But he never agreed with the way coach Brian Smith steered his sides, so he just walked away and went travelling around the country. When he came back, he started pulling beers in a pub, even going on to own a pub, and then became an electrician.

That was an eye-opener, from an early age, about what

was important in life. I felt grounded, like I had options in life. It meant I never had any vision in my head of embarking on a long footy career that ended when my body couldn't allow me to go any longer. Watching Gav and his experiences meant I was never going to be a rugby league tragic.

But that didn't mean I didn't love playing it. It took me three months away from the game to realise how much I missed it. And I'll be honest: with the money being offered, it was a great opportunity. Mum called all of the managers who had been interested. 'Look, Mark's just playing it as a game now,' she told them. 'When and if the time comes that we do need a manager, I'll ring every one of you and give you an opportunity.' Then we signed a two-year deal with the Dragons.

Mum wasn't the only one who was important during those years. If I didn't stay in school, I wouldn't be able to play Australian Schoolboys. The lovely career advisor at Peakhurst High, Miss Edwards, sat me down. 'What do you want to do with your life?' she asked. 'I want to play footy for a living,' was the reply. She really helped me through the next two years to my HSC, making sure I met what was required by the curriculum.

If I hadn't had her there, making sure I attended school and did the right thing, I would've been kicked out. Who knows what influence that would've had on my footy.

The decision to stay in school paid off. In 1998, I was playing Jersey Flegg (under-20s) for St George at the age of 16. Peter O'Sullivan, who is now a recruitment manager for the Roosters, was the coach. He had a lot of faith in me. It culminated in my selection for Australian Schoolboys, which was always the stepping stone to bigger things. There were some players in that side who really kicked on and became big names: Mark Riddell, Ashley Harrison, Luke Burt, Brent Kite and the always entertaining Brett Finch. When I arrived back in Australia from the overseas tour, the Dragons were keen to renew my deal. Mum stayed true to her word and phoned every single manager who had been good enough to show some interest in signing me, inviting them over to our house to listen to what they had to say. She'll always do the right thing by everyone. She's just a real honest person.

We signed with George Mimis from SFX Sports, and soon after we did a new two-year deal with the Dragons.

It was around this time that the surname really started to generate a bit of press. And it was an easy story: Uncle Reg was a centre, I was a centre, although when I first came into grade they slotted me into full-back because I was too lean. If I was going to make it in the centres, I was going to have to put on some more weight or I'd be trampled.

I didn't pay as much attention to the talk about being Reg Gasnier's nephew as other people did. It put absolutely no pressure on me. Some players coming through feel the weight of their surname, especially those who have followed in their father's footsteps. But there were so many years and generations between the time when Uncle Reg played and when I started coming on. Each time I made a rep team, I never heard, 'You only made it because your name's Gasnier.' To be honest, I can only remember one or two sledges on the field.

And the more I played, the more fans noticed me in my own right. After the Jersey Flegg season finished, I played the rest of the season in President's Cup, which is better known as third grade.

One day, after a game during that 1998 season, one supporter came up and said, 'You know, I hope you get your opportunity.' He pushed a jersey and a pen under my nose. He wanted an autograph – my first one.

He didn't want it because of my surname, but because he liked the way I played. 'You're my favourite player,' he said. 'This signature will be worth something in a bit of time – so I want you to take this and sign it now.'

THREE

SPECIAL NIGHT

Ask any player who's ever played at the old Marathon Stadium, the Newcastle Knights' home ground before it was refurbished a few years ago, and they'll tell you there was hardly a tougher road trip. The sign on the wall of the tunnel when you came out of the away dressing-room made it very clear: THIS IS NEWCASTLE.

It really was a graveyard. As legend has it, it was the place where the Knights' coaches would ask the grounds staff to hose out the away dressing-room so every inch of it was soaking wet when the opposition arrived. It's also claimed that they marked the sidelines two metres inside where they were supposed to be to suit the bash-and-barge game of the Knights' forwards.

It might not be part of Marathon Stadium legend, but it's a special place for me because it's where my first-grade career sparked, out of nowhere and unplanned. It was 24 March 2000. Round 8. Friday night footy. Newcastle featured players like Andrew and Matthew Johns, Ben Kennedy, Billy Peden, Timana Tahu, Tony Butterfield and Robbie O'Davis.

I'd just played a full match of Premier League and was back in the sheds when I received the call. The worst thing about that dressing-room, as any player from that time will remember, were the showers. They were just taps on the end of some pipes, which you twisted and some cold water would dribble out. I was normally always the last in the shower, so sometimes I didn't even bother. If you're having a few beers on the bus on the way home anyway, who really cares?

Not that I'm complaining. I used to like that side of the game. Always did. Even when I was playing rugby in France, I loved the old rural grounds. It was just like being back when I was a kid and playing for Renown United, when all that mattered was the match and playing with your mates. But on this night in Newcastle I managed to get a shower, and I was out in the small room to the side that reserve grade inhabits while first grade gets ready to play.

I was getting changed, grinning at what the 13,000 or so people outside really thought of us. We knew this because there was a window in the corner of the room, which had been smashed in, and we were literally sitting beneath the feet of the fans in the main grandstand above. It allowed the Knights' faithful to look in and yell out whatever they wanted.

'Youse are going to lose, Dragons!' 'You can't play!' That type of stuff – and some other colourful words I won't repeat.

It was full on. Much different to what footy grounds are like these days.

I was sitting there when first grade's co-coach Andrew Farrar came up to me.

'Gaz!' he said, surprising me. 'What are you doing?'

'I'm getting changed, mate,' I said, confused. 'What do you think?'

'Well, do you want to play?'

'What? *Tonight?*'

'Do you want to play or don't you?'

'Yeah!' I couldn't believe what was happening.

'Get your boots on.'

My chance to play first grade had been presented to me because Matt Cooper had gone down with a back injury during the warm-up.

Andrew, or 'Pops' as he was known to all of us around the club, had been out there on the field, and I'm pretty sure he'd made the decision on his own, without consulting David Waite, his fellow coach. He just walked in and told me how it was going to be.

I heard later that sideline commentator Andrew Voss said that I was so nervous that I couldn't put my boots on – I was shaking that much. That's a load of crap. I couldn't wait. That was my moment. My big chance.

The previous year was when things got really serious. I'd played a handful of SG Ball matches, but then Peter O'Sullivan pretty much had me full-time in the under-20s and then into Premier League.

I thought I was nearly ready to make the big leap into first grade. David Waite and the rest of the coaching staff had other ideas. David pulled me into his office one day, sat me down and gave it to me straight. I never had a whole lot do with Waitey during his time at the Dragons, but what he told me that day had a profound influence on my career, and my life.

'Gaz, you know, I think you're ready for first grade now,' he said to me. 'You've got all the skills to play at that level, but you won't handle the physicality of it. You're too small. Until you put on eight or nine kilos, you won't play first grade. If you want to have a proper crack at this, it's time to get serious.'

It sunk in there and then. Those words were just what I needed to hear, and they were lodged in my head throughout the next 12 months as I chased the dream. I went away for my second year of Australian Schoolboys, through England, Ireland and France, and again it was with some future super-stars of the game, blokes like Justin Hodges, Jamie Lyon, Brent Tate.

I'd done some work in the gym before going away, of course, but when I came back I ramped it right up. I trained my arse off and it was one of the hardest things I've done. Putting on nine kilograms of muscle isn't easy, but I did it and it taught me a very valuable lesson: to make it at the top level you need to train the house down. You need a really strong work ethic.

This was 1999, the year when the Dragons became more than St George. They had become St George Illawarra fol-lowing the momentous decision post-Super League to merge with Illawarra.

Because the salary cap rules had been relaxed as an

incentive for merged clubs, there were stars everywhere during a pre-season camp in Orange, which was as much about getting to know each other as anything.

There were blokes from both sides of the joint venture who had I grown up watching. On the St George side, there were players like Mark Coyne, Wayne Bartrim, Nathan Blacklock, Anthony Mundine and Brad Mackay. From the Illawarra side of the ledger, there was Andrew Hart, Shaun Timmins, Craig Smith, Rod Wishart and Trent Barrett.

Then there was Mary... Paul McGregor played in the centres and was big and fit and strong and stepped around defenders as good as anyone else in the competition. He was one of my footballing heroes, so much so that I would get nervous just saying hello to him, which is silly because he is as nice and decent as you could want.

There were a few other young players in that camp who would go on to wear the Red V with distinction: Matt Cooper, Jason Ryles and Luke Bailey. I'm not sure about them, but being part of that camp made me think, *This is where I want to be.*

That inaugural season saw us divide our time between Wollongong and Sydney. The St George boys would assemble at St George Leagues Club and go down to Wollongong two days a week. Then the players based in Wollongong would come and train at Kogarah Oval two days a week.

I mightn't have played any first-grade footy that year, but I realised that your career wasn't all based on a natural ability to play football. It showed me you had to work hard, and it also showed me that you had to have some humility.

Mark Coyne, more than anyone, taught me that. He had

played in Grand Finals for St George, and won State of Origins for Queensland with last-minute tries. He had played for his country, too, but in 1999 he was dropped to Premier League against North Sydney.

Instead of being bitter about the drop to reserve grade, he accepted it. And if he was bitter, he didn't show it. He came up to me at training that week, shook my hand and introduced himself. It concerns me there is no such thing as reserve grade any longer, because it teaches young footballers the importance of keeping your feet on the ground and allows them to play with seasoned first graders.

Coynie was the one I felt for the most at the end of that season, when we lost the Grand Final to Melbourne. He retired after that match and deserved to go out in a better way. That defeat – when the Storm won the premiership with a penalty try in the last two minutes – only added to the Dragons' pressure to end the Grand Final drought, even if it was the merged club's first season. The pressure kept building and building over the next decade.

That's scrutiny from the outside, though. The Grand Final loss really hurt, especially the older blokes like Trent Barrett and Shaun Timmins but, as a footballer knows, whatever scars you pick up one season are soon forgotten by the start of the next. What use is there in dragging your bottom lip? It doesn't get you anywhere.

I know this might sound disrespectful, but I didn't give a shit what was happening around me. I just wanted to train hard, get a shot at first grade and then make the most of it.

And that shot came when Matt Cooper went down in the warm-up at Marathon Stadium. After the game, Andrew Farrar spoke to the press about the confusion over who to bring in. He could've gone for Lee Hookey or Lee Murphy. 'If Gaz wasn't in the room at the time, it might have been someone else,' he said to some reporters later that night.

After telling me to get ready to play, Pops told me the plan: I would slot onto the replacement bench and then come on after 20 minutes with Jason Hooper switching from the wing into the backrow.

Like Andrew Voss, there were some watching at home who reckoned I looked nervous whenever the camera flashed to my 18-year-old head on the sideline. Nothing could've been further from the truth. I was just excited to get on the field. Then, just as Pops had said, I came on after 20 minutes.

It turned into a thriller, a lateral game with plenty of ball movement. We were desperate. Three weeks earlier, we'd been humiliated 70–10 by the Storm in a replay of the Grand Final. Our form had been so bad, and the Knights hadn't been beaten at home so far that season. But we dug deep, played some solid footy, and with 11 minutes to go we led 13–12 thanks to a Trent Barrett field goal earlier in the match.

Then the Knights shifted play towards the right side of the field, where I was defending on the wing outside of Shaun Timmins. Knights centre Mark Hughes came our way, right towards the small gap between the pair of us. I wedged in on Timmo, trying to close the gap. I should've known better.

If I'd played with him before I *would've* known Shaun Timmins doesn't miss a tackle. Hughes passed to winger Lenny Beckett, who scored in the corner. Andrew Johns kicked the conversion out wide for an 18–13 lead.

There was one abiding thought in my head: *fuck*. A mistake like that feels bad at the best of times. But on debut?

I'd played all right up until that point. Nothing fancy, just a lot of dummy half runs. The Johns boys had tried to rattle me with the cross-field bombs, but I'd taken all of them without any fuss. The important thing was that I was comfortable. I didn't feel intimidated. I never felt out of place, even if it was all new to me.

So here I was, praying for an opportunity – anything! – to erase the mess I had just created. I was looking for redemption. I didn't think it would come from the kick-off, when Knights replacement prop Glenn Grief knocked on. Within three tackles we were within striking distance. Jamie Ainscough ran out of dummy half, the ball came to me and I stretched out with everything I had, and got the ball down in the corner. Wayne Bartrim landed the conversion from the sideline to give us a 19–18 lead, before Jamie scored again on the way to a 25–18 win.

You can imagine the relief, and it wasn't just scoring the try. I'm grateful for the way my debut came about. I didn't have a week to mull over in my head how I was going to play it or deal with the hype and media attention about the debut of Reg Gasnier's nephew.

If there was one bloke who could attract a whole heap of headlines on his own, it was our five-eighth, Anthony 'Choc' Mundine. A fortnight after making my debut, as I was starting to find my feet in the top grade, I turned up to training at Kogarah one morning to find half of Sydney's media there.

Choc had vanished, apparently off to America because he was unhappy with the game. His good friend Solomon Haumono had done something similar while playing for Canterbury two years earlier: he left in the dead of night and went to London in search of his girlfriend, Gabrielle Richens, aka 'The Pleasure Machine'. When Choc returned, he announced his retirement from rugby league to take up a career in boxing.

I know Choc received a lot of criticism from Dragons fans after walking out of the club, but I can't help but like the guy. He played with my brother Gav, and apart from the fact that he is a freak of an athlete, I always thought he was a champion bloke. A lot of people don't realise his generosity. Of course he gives a lot of his time to young Indigenous kids, but I've seen him with people from all walks of life. He gives away his socks and boots – everything he has.

When he took up boxing and started with the trash talk, the Dragons players and I would laugh our heads off. 'Oh, what about that bloody Mundine?' people would ask, and we'd set the record straight: 'No, no, he's a good fella.'

Mundine's last game was against the Roosters in Wollongong, but I remember the occasion for something else. The stress of playing first grade had given me shingles, and the rash was noticeable on the side of my neck. It was so conspicuous that I had to stand to one side in my brother's wedding photo, taken the day before the game.

I didn't dare tell the coaching staff or team doctor what was happening. I'd only played two games and I didn't want to give away my position, because it might've been another six or seven months before I got it back.

For the next two months I started every match, either on the wing so Jamie Ainscough or Shaun Timmins could play in the centres, or in the centres with either of them.

Then my debut season, after I had played eight matches, ended in a heartbeat. It was May 14 – Mothers' Day – at Parramatta Stadium. Big Eels forward Nathan Hindmarsh ran at me and his knee went straight through my shin, snapping my leg. It was my first major injury. If only it was the last.

FOUR

MARY

IT's NOT EVERY DAY you get to meet your footballing hero. It's not every day you get to find out he's not just the champion player you always loved watching, but an equally good person. And then it's not every day that you get to play alongside and learn from him.

I never thought I'd have the opportunity to play with Paul 'Mary' McGregor, even as I got to know him. I had met Paul in 1999 when he was the inaugural captain of the St George and Illawarra joint venture. The top 25 players in the squad, plus a few up-and-coming players like Matt Cooper, Benny Hornby, Jason Ryles, Luke Bailey and myself, were allowed to attend a pre-season camp in Orange, and I was put in a cabin with the Illawarra Steelers boys. Although nervous at first, it turned out to be a great experience, and that's where I met Mary.

In 1999 the reserve grade teams kept their pre-merger identities and actually competed against each other. I was still at school that year but lucky enough to be playing reserve grade, and the week we were meant to play the Steelers, Mary was playing because he was returning from injury. Thank God it was selections for Australian Schoolboys that week and I didn't have to go up against him, although it would have been a good lesson.

When I broke my leg the following season, and the Dragons finished in ninth spot and out of the finals, I learnt that the team's traditional Mad Monday celebrations kicked off at Coalcliff and then we'd do a pub crawl back towards Wollongong. Mary was also a hero to the Illawarra boys – a real father figure – so on our way up to Coalcliff the boys decided he should be with us, even though he had just retired. 'Let's go past Eagle's house,' someone said. (Eagle was his other nickname, after the bald eagle.) He was building his house near Towradgi, where he still lives today, and as the bus drove past he was on the building site, labouring for the builders.

'Eagle, get on!' we ordered. 'It's Mad Monday!' It took him half a second to down tools and jump on the bus.

As the day unfolded, I ended up getting into a shout with Mary, and that was my first mistake – I didn't know Mary could drink so well. But I was determined to keep pace with him until the death because I admired him so much. I ended up staying with him at his house that night. He's since become one of my closest friends, along with his wife, Nicole, and kids, Demi and Kade, who I've seen grow up. You don't plan friendships like that, of course. Just because you admire someone doesn't mean that you're going to get along like a house on fire. But Mary and his family are genuinely some of the nicest people you'll ever meet.

Looking back, that was the best thing about St George Illawarra. It was a merged team that had played just two seasons together, but the environment they created was very relaxed. That was as important as anything to playing some decent footy, which was something I was determined to do in 2001 because of how things had ended the previous season. Because I'd only played eight games, I felt like I was going right back to where I started. I feared I would be toiling away in reserve grade, trying to prove myself again.

To the credit of Andrew Farrar, that never happened. During the off-season, with my broken leg healed, I put on more muscle weight and started tipping the scales at about 98 kilograms, maybe a tad more.

Then Pops pulled me aside one day early into our pre-season. He told me that Mary was coming out of retirement to play centre as Shaun Timmins's knee troubles continued and he would be out for the season. I would be playing left centre, and I could learn a lot from having Mary around. For as long as I could remember, I had always played at right centre. A bit of five-eighth or full-back here or there in the lower grades, but always on the right. It didn't matter. I was just ecstatic to be part of the team and given the opportunity.

Mary was the reason why I loved watching the Steelers when I was a kid. He was a right centre and I was a right centre, and I loved his skill and evasiveness for a big man who stood at 192 centimetres and weighed 100 kilograms. Mary had the level of skill to pop up anywhere on the field and be a threat to off-load or set another player up, which I wanted to emulate. I admired him more than any other player.

Throughout that 2001 season I couldn't tell you any specific advice that he imparted to help me. I think it showed a level of respect that he never told me to 'do this, do that'. He would pull me aside at training and talk about different scenarios in a game that he could remember from experience, and us young blokes would feed on that type of individual attention.

He was a calming influence more than anything and, just like those Illawarra blokes, he became a father figure for me that year, along with Trent Barrett and Shaun Timmins.

I've no doubt that he was a big reason why I managed to play a full season in 2001 – 28 games in total for 11 tries. We finished the home-and-away season in seventh position and were confident of what we could achieve in the finals, even if the Parramatta side that year was in superb form, breaking records all over the place.

In the first week of the finals we met the Bulldogs at the Sydney Showground, and it took a Willie Peters field goal to seal a 23–22 win and send us through to the second week. We weren't so lucky against the Broncos in the semifinal at the Sydney Football Stadium and lost 44–28.

Despite the disappointment of losing so deep into the finals, my form that year was strong enough to earn some representative jumpers, well before I expected to wear them. I played for City Origin in their annual clash against Country in April, but the real shock came when I was named in the Australian squad to tour England.

That was the year of the September 11 terrorist attacks on the World Trade Center and the Pentagon, and it sent shockwaves all around the world, heightening anxieties about air travel. When the Tri Nations tour of England came to being picked, under national coach Chris Anderson, there were real concerns from some players about going, particularly Broncos prop Shane Webcke. I could understand if some were reluctant to fly, particularly those players with kids. But I was more than happy to go.

The tour was going to be cancelled altogether before a truncated tour of just three matches was put forward. I never played in any of those matches against Great Britain, but I did manage to play in a lead-up Test against Papua New Guinea in Port Moresby, in which I scored a try.

Above all, I got the chance to play alongside some of the all-time legends of the code, like Brad Fittler, Andrew Johns and Darren Lockyer. And I put much of that opportunity to Andrew Farrar for having belief in me and the influence of guys like Mary, Timmo and Baz around me. At one point during that breakthrough season I signed a decent deal to stay at the Dragons. I won't lie: there were bigger offers to go elsewhere, but I stayed because I loved it. I didn't want to go anywhere else. I couldn't play for anyone else. Everything I learnt from all of the players I've mentioned also played a significant part in knowing where I belonged.

Although Mary retired for good that year, he and his family are still like family to me to this day.

FIVE

THE RED V

We were walking from the ground at WIN Stadium, heads down. We had stayed with Manly for much of the game. Midway through the second half it had been 12 all. As we left the field, the scoreboard told the sorry tale: they'd won 38–12.

I could tell Trent Barrett, our captain, was cranky. Really cranky.

'Baz, are you all right, mate?' I asked him.

'No,' he fumed. 'Didn't you see what happened? Fucking Browny – he slapped me. He fucking slapped me.'

'What? Are you serious?' I couldn't believe what I was hearing.

As I soon found out – and as the rugby league world had seen live on television – our coach, Nathan Brown, had slapped our captain on the sideline earlier in the match.

Manly were about to do a goal line drop-out in the 53rd

41

minute, and I was walking back to my usual spot. Lance Thompson walked past me and I was waiting for the kick, looking towards the goal posts, when there was a huge roar from the crowd.

Nathan, in his second year as coach but still only 29 years old, had pulled Thommo, Baz and our half-back, Brett Firman, to the side of the field and was barking out instructions. He slapped Trent in the heat of making his point, and after Lance tried to turn and walk away the coach grabbed him and dragged him back by the sleeve. When I eventually saw the replay, I was stunned.

That was April 2003, and it was a dark day for all of us. The NRL ended up fining Nathan $5000, but deep down I knew it could've been far worse. Trent Barrett had become such an influential figure in the club that he probably could've ruined Browny's career right there and then. He could've complained to management or quietly turned the players against the coach. Blokes who aren't as strong as Trent probably would've done it.

As a sign of the man he is, he didn't. He just said, 'Browny, I understand you're new to coaching . . . but if you do that again, I'll knock you out.'

You've got to remember that coaches are under a lot of pressure. They spend so much time on game plans – week in, week out – and watching so much video that they want you to play a certain way. We weren't playing up to the level he wanted, and the game was there to be taken.

To Browny's credit, though, he said to us at the next training session, 'Look, I definitely shouldn't have done that.

I was out of line. I got caught up in the heat of the moment, so I apologise.'

Then it was all forgotten. Trent didn't hold a grudge against Browny; it was never raised again.

We can all laugh about it now. The look on Firmo's face is priceless. He was in no-man's land. It's like he's thinking: *Did you just slap Trent?* And it would've been funny to see what would have happened if he'd slapped Lance.

At the time it was pretty tough to play for the Dragons, for a whole heap of reasons. The 2002 and 2003 seasons were massive frustrations for me personally because of injury. I didn't know it then, but they weren't going to be the only seasons with an asterisk next them because of problems with my body.

In 2002 it was a dislocated foot in round five against Parramatta that kept me to only 14 games. I went in to make a tackle and all the pressure went back on my foot. The ligament between my big toe and one next to it snapped. I also chipped a bit of bone. You're normally meant to get an operation, but the medical staff were confident that it could repair without it. It still took a few months to heal and rehab.

In 2003 it was a series of hammy, quad and calf tears that limited me to just 13 matches for the season. I have no doubt that those two seasons hurt my career in the long run, I was young and raw and coming off a very good 2001 season that had ended in Australian selection. I missed out on playing for NSW and Australia during those years, but it wasn't the omission that ate at me the most, it was the fact that I felt fitter and stronger than ever when I was injury free. For the first time I felt a sense of belonging within the group at the Dragons, a belief that I had earnt my stripes.

Meanwhile, Nathan Brown had his own pressures. He had been appointed coach to replace Andrew Farrar in 2003. Nathan had been a legendary St George hooker, with his curly blond hair, who had been forced to retire in early 2001 because of a congenital neck problem that was found after he was injured during a trial match. When he first got the job he was only 28 – the youngest in the history of the game.

But I reckon the bloke who copped it the most was Trent Barrett. Because of the great history of the club – of the St George club – there was a lot of animosity towards him since he had come from the Illawarra side of the merger. There had also been a lot of tension around who was going to play half-back and who was going to play five-eighth – Baz or Anthony Mundine – when the two clubs came together. When Mundine left, Barrett slotted back into his familiar role at five-eighth, and I think much of the drama stemmed from there.

For all the criticism directed at his game, which was rubbish because he was such a talented player (the best five-eighth I've played with, in fact), the thing that stunned me the most were the personal attacks. Inevitably, I was dragged into it. There used to be rumours once a year along the lines that I was sleeping with Trent's wife. Jason Ryles was pulled into it there for a while. We don't know where the lies came from, but once a year someone out there in the rugby league world would try to upset the team.

It's like anything, really: when you know it's not true, it's not that hard to forget about it.

That said, I did come out in the press at one stage and say, 'I'm sick and tired of the innuendo that relates to fall outs and a number of things involving me and my teammates and the club.'

This is the part of playing rugby league, and playing for a high-profile club, that was frustrating. I was often on the phone straightaway to my family to set the record straight. When Mum would read in the paper that Trent and I had fallen out, she would call.

'You and Trent are close, aren't you?' she would ask.

'Of course we are, Mum,' I would have to say. 'Don't listen to it.'

Baz and I would have a laugh – that was one good thing about it. Once, before a match against the Warriors in early 2004 that Baz had pulled out of with an injury, I had to set the record straight again.

'No way have I had a blow-up with Trent,' I told *The Daily Telegraph*. 'Baz is easily one of my best mates in the team, and I remember two years ago there was another rumour getting around the traps that I had a fight with him. It makes you really angry how these things start. I mean, I was up at Trent's place on Friday night having a barbecue, and he was receiving the same phone calls about a fight and this and that. But it couldn't be any further from the truth.'

Baz also chimed in. 'We're a very close group of players

and it's a harmonious club. It's rubbish to suggest anything else.'

Sometimes the criticism of Baz came from people who you would least expect it. When Trent was about to leave the club to play in England, the pressure hit its peak when Johnny Raper – an Immortal of the game and a club legend – said Trent wasn't fit to wear the Dragons crest on his chest.

'There is a bloke there who is not putting in,' he told a stunned audience at a function in Newcastle. 'He wears the No.6, but if I had my way, he would not be in the team. He forgets the thing that is sitting over the top of his left tit. It's the St George Dragons crest, and he is not fit to wear it on his chest.'

I thought that was very disrespectful for a player who had done so much for the club, had won a Dally M Medal and played for his state and country. People don't understand that sometimes you have a bad game, but it's not for lack of effort. Sometimes you're in a form slump, other times things don't go your way. But I've always thought Trent's effort was there. That's all you can ask of your teammates: that they try their guts out.

The other thing with Baz is that you couldn't meet a nicer person. The same applies to his wife, Kylie, and their lovely family. I really felt for him throughout that whole period – we all did. He never deserved it. All I know is that there was hardly another player who had a bigger influence on my career.

The reason we were hammered outside of our club, and even by our own supporters, is that so many people thought we were underachievers. 'Well, they should have won a comp by now,' was a common line we heard. That's when the dreaded C-word started to get some airplay for the first time: Chokers.

The merged club of St George Illawarra had lost a Grand Final, but there had been four others lost titles for the long-suffering St George fans since 1979. We had a very experienced roster when the clubs came together, with a salary cap of about $7.2 million, but over the years that followed the cap had to almost halve to where everyone else's was: $3.25 million.

When you looked at our team, we had talent to burn: Luke Bailey and Jason Ryles up front. Mark Riddell at hooker. Benny Creagh had made his debut in 2003 and was a star in the making. Lance Thompson. Shaun Timmins. Benny Hornby. Trent Barrett. Matt Cooper.

We were getting to a point when it was going to become hard to keep all of our stars. Sensing an opportunity, that's when overseas clubs started to circle.

As that 2003 season unfolded, there was interest from UK Super League powerhouses St Helens and Wigan about signing me. The talks between the clubs and my manager, George Mimis, were going on for months, and there was a lot of speculation in the press. It was the first time I had ever been pursued so heavily about leaving.

In the end, I ended up re-signing with the Dragons for three years – through the end of 2006 – even though I could've earned three times more money at Wigan. I fronted the media about my decision:

'I sat down with my family and girlfriend before deciding. It just wasn't worth it. I think if I had gone over there and played football, I would have regretted it. I didn't want to have that feeling. It was a very lucrative offer and I probably wouldn't rule out going over there towards the end of my career. Maurice Lindsay [former chairman of Wigan] was very nice in his dealings and came across as a very nice person, and it would be a great club.'

I know in my heart I could never have left. I was 22, had 62 matches for the Dragons since making my first-grade debut as an 18-year-old in 2000, and scored 36 tries. There was still so much more I wanted to achieve, wearing the Red V of the Dragons, the sky-blue of NSW and the green and gold of Australia. I wasn't ready to walk away from that.

By March the next year, however, things were starting to weigh on me. I didn't know what I wanted from the game – or if I wanted to play at all. My form wavered and the club gave me a weekend off, but I came back in Premier League against Newtown at Henson Park. After the match, a reporter from *The Sunday Telegraph* approached me.

'I'll see how I go,' I said. 'If I'm ready next week I'll play, but if I'm not ready I won't.' I admitted I was 'still searching for a bit of enthusiasm'. Asked if my mental approach to the game was a hundred percent, I replied, 'No way. That's the only thing I'm worried about because I think that makes up 80 per cent of the play.'

All this was crap, though, truth be known. I was having some issues in my personal life, and still to this day only my mother knows what they were. I went through a few media interviews like this. You sometimes have to offer excuses, or a deviation from the truth, but you also have to cop the criticism and speculation that comes with those excuses. I definitely learnt that throughout my career.

The speculation into my disillusionment with the game made me think about my commitment. If I am perfectly honest, I did not live and breathe footy. Early on, I did it for the money – or at least I thought I did. But after a few grueling off-seasons, I realised I was bullshitting myself. I didn't live and breathe football – I still don't – but what I *did* want to achieve was to be the best in my position and the best teammate possible.

Baz was important during that time, despite the stupid rumours that constantly whirled around about us not getting on. He was one of the main reasons I kept going. He told me that he had been through rough patches during his career, and assured me that things would turn around.

A lack of maturity held me back from being honest with myself, or maybe I didn't want to put my balls on the line and say it out loud. Either way, I was too naive to know at this age.

My dad always made us work hard from a young age. I was never afraid of the possibility that I would have to go into the workforce. A lot of people said throughout my career that I could walk away from rugby league at any time.

It was never any disrespect to the game, nor was it ever a case of taking my luck of being a first-grade footballer for granted.

I was just being me.

SIX

FIRE UP

I KNOW THEY ARE the two words that will follow me for the rest of my life, just as they followed me for much of my career. After the incident, people on the street would yell the words out to me. Even kids would say the phrase, although I prayed they didn't know what it was all about. There were T-shirts made up, banners on the hill at Kogarah and Wollongong – wherever we were playing. Years later, people would mention it if they spotted me in a bar, and it would often become a conversation starter. I suspect you know the two words I am speaking about: 'Fire up'. I should copyright them.

I was itching to play a part in the 2004 State of Origin series. Injuries had already denied me the chance to wear the sky-blue of New South Wales during the last two seasons. It was during the camp with the Kangaroos at the end of 2001 that I started to crave a state representative start. 'Origin's as good as it gets,' some of the boys said, which was no dis-respect to the Australian jumper but an indication of just how good Origin is, and the Blues were coming off a series win against Queensland the previous year. So when I was selected in May 2004 to play in Phil Gould's NSW team, I was ecstatic.

For that first game, I was selected at left centre with Matt Gidley from Newcastle on the right. And while I wasn't going to play on my preferred side of the field, I was happy to be alongside my Dragons teammates. Ben Hornby, who had been selected ahead of Anthony Minichiello from the Roosters, was at full-back, pushing Mini out to the left wing. Shaun Timmins, who had overcome two serious knee inju-ries that threatened his career, was picked at five-eighth; and Brent Kite was the starting prop.

It should've been the happiest week of my life. But then, within the space of just a couple of days, it spun wildly out of control, unravelling like I could never have imagined. Of all the highs and lows I've gone through in the life, this was one of the lowest. Because it had been my mistake.

The first inkling that something had gone wrong came the day after our very large bonding session on the Tuesday night after we had come into camp at the Crowne Plaza in Coogee earlier that day. On Wednesday afternoon, nurs-ing a pretty big hangover, the team's media manager, Polly McCardell, came and saw Mini and me in our room. Playing on the left side, we had been partnered as roommates.

'Look, Mini, we've got a report from a girl that you've left a rude message on her phone,' she told us.

'It can't be, Polly,' Mini said, defending himself. 'Because I lost my phone.' Which he had.

'Where did you lose it? What time did you lose it?'

'I don't know. I went to Star City and I lost it there.'

Straightaway, Mini and I assumed that some random bloke had found Mini's phone at the casino and started making prank calls on it.

The next day, the story came out in *The Daily Telegraph* that an obscene phone message had been left on the voicemail of a 27-year-old woman at 3.41 am the previous morning. As the day progressed, the witch-hunt was on to find out who'd made the call. I was sitting around in a café in Coogee with Mini, Shaun Timmins and Craig Fitzgibbon. 'It could be me,' I said to them. I knew it had been a big night, and I had forgotten a lot of what had happened. 'But, boys, I don't remember leaving that message.'

At two o'clock that afternoon, the team assembled in the foyer. We were about to walk out the door for training at Wentworth Park when one of the team officials yelled out to me: 'Gaz, Carry wants to see you in his room.' 'Carry' is Geoff Carr, Chief Executive of the NSW and Australian rugby leagues, who has been around the game for decades.

That's when I knew. I knew straightaway that it was me. All I needed was confirmation.

Geoff sat me down and played a recording of the message. '[Woman's name], where the f*** are you?' the voice on the tape said. 'There's four toey humans in the cab – it's twenty to four. Our c**** are fat and f****** ready to spurt sauce, and you're in bed. F*** me – fire up, you sad c***.'

'Is this you?' Geoff asked.

'Mate, it sounds like it, yeah . . . It sounds like me,' I replied.

'You don't remember doing it?' he asked.

'No, but obviously it is, because that's my voice.'

'Mate, well, sorry – we're going to have to let you go,' he said.

'For what?' I replied, shocked and confused.

'You're sacked,' Geoff said. 'Grab your stuff and ring your manager.'

Before I knew it, I was crouching down in the passenger seat of a car as it sped out of the Crowne Plaza car park, giving the media pack assembled out front the slip. It didn't take long for them to put two and two together. Once all the boys were at training, and I was missing, it was obvious that I had been the one who had made the phone call.

To this very day, I still don't remember making it. And the reason is pretty obvious: I was very drunk. I don't remember the call. I definitely don't remember the whole night . . .

We had come into camp at the Crowne Plaza eight days before the first match of the Origin series at the Olympic Stadium at Homebush in Sydney.

After a kids' clinic at St Mary's in the western suburbs, we started off with dinner at St Mary's Rugby League Club and then stopped for a few drinks at the Colyton Hotel.

When the team bus hit the eastern suburbs, we split up:

the forwards were off to the Charing Cross Hotel in Waverley and the backs to the Clovelly Hotel, just north of where we were staying.

It was important that we got to know each other because it was a relatively new team. Gus knew the value and importance of this – he'd been there and done all of it at the elite level before – and he had set some clear rules. You couldn't talk to your teammates from your own club. If you did, it was a two-finger skol of your beer.

The term 'bonding session' is a dirty word these days, but I don't care what anyone says: when you get out and have a few beers, players *do* bond. It relaxes them, it breaks barriers.

After the Clovelly shut, we headed back towards the Coogee Bay Hotel, and that's where things get a little hazy for me. By the time it got to 3 am, Gus wanted us all to go home. So we headed back to the Crowne Plaza.

From here I only remember bits and pieces, but I do know there was a heap of us who decided to head back out.

I'm not giving anyone up, because it was well publicised that Craig Gower, Craig Wing, Willie Mason, Anthony Minichiello and Mark O'Meley were among those of us who headed out. It all came out in forensic detail. We spilt up into two groups, heading off in separate taxis. Some went to the casino, while the rest of us pretty much tried to get into every nightclub in Sydney, from Kings Cross to Oxford Street.

Trent Waterhouse, Mace and I went to Leichhardt, trying to find a club we had heard was still open. I spotted a bakery – I was starving – and stood there on Parramatta Road eating a pie. There would've been a hundred people going to work who saw us. We waited for a taxi, couldn't get one, so we ended up on a bus that was headed towards the city. That probably wasn't the smartest thing to do.

There are so many things that came up from that night that I don't recall being a part of. There was CCTV footage handed out all over the place. There were images of us mucking around with the bouncers at the Empire Hotel in Kings Cross, players tackling each other as we went on our way.

In hindsight, I wonder why. The media had a field day with it, and with me they had a face to put to the scandal. I've no doubt that we were copping the frustrations of the public over other things that had happened earlier that year.

The Bulldogs rape scandal in Coffs Harbour – from which no charges were laid – had occurred in February. Now the representative season had been gobbled up with more adverse headlines involving rugby league players and women, right at the time when the game's showcase event was about to kick off.

Now that I'm older and understand a bit more how things work, I can't blame the media. I'm not saying we copped the blame for things we didn't do, but we bore the brunt of the public's frustration and the officials' wrath because of other incidents and scandals that had engulfed the game.

There was also one newspaper report that said Mace and I and others had gone to a brothel. I was prepared to cop the voicemail message, but, no, I would not accept the brothel claim. My manager and I even considered taking legal action. In the end we didn't, because I thought: *what's the point?* It just drags everything out into the public light again, reminding everyone of what you did.

You don't want damages for defamation anyway. You just want your credibility back. For me, the best way to do that was to shut my mouth and get back to playing football.

But as that Thursday afternoon played out, after I had been sacked by Geoff Carr, it became unclear when that would actually be.

Coming back to St George Leagues Club, across the road from Kogarah Oval, was the worst part about the whole ordeal. Some of my teammates were there, asking what had happened. Then Peter Doust pulled me into the boardroom and asked the same question. 'Mate, I was blind drunk; I don't remember doing it,' I said to him. 'Not that it makes it any better.'

I will never forget walking out the front of the St George Leagues Club and the huge media scrum waiting for me. That's when it hit me: the enormity of what I'd done, the consequences of one silly action on the drink.

'I will make contact with the person to personally apologise,' I said, nervously reading from a prepared statement. 'I was under the influence of alcohol, but I understand I have to be responsible for my actions. I have paid a huge price for my actions in the circumstances. It has been my life's ambition to play State of Origin.'

Back inside the leagues club there was more to come. 'Well,' Dousty began, 'you'll be stood down indefinitely until the Board meets.' From there he came down hard on me about the importance of my behaviour, my surroundings and who I represented. But I still knew he genuinely cared about how I was feeling. Later, the Dragons' board decided to stand me down for a match and fine me $50,000. In the final wash-up, Mini was also sacked from the Blues, while Mason ($6000), Waterhouse ($5000) and Wing, O'Meley and Gower ($3000 each) were also fined.

It wasn't the money that hurt me most, but the suspension – all I could think about was playing again.

After I left the leagues club, I had to speak to my girlfriend of the past five years, Cherie McKenzie, and her mother, Di. That conversation wasn't easy either. 'Look, you're a young boy,' Di said. 'You do stupid things, but maybe it's a lesson learnt.' She was as good as she could be, while also trying to get her point across that I had hurt her daughter.

The worst part of it all was facing Mum. She had come to the leagues club late, after I had read the statement, and to see her crying was the lowest point. I could handle the public scrutiny, the media attention, even whatever the media wanted to write. You can live with that because you know the truth. But your family has to share your burden as well.

The *only* saving grace was that my family knows my character, they know the person who others out there might still be questioning, even as they read this book. They know what I'm like, they know me, and they've seen me enough on the drink to realise that I muck around a lot. There was no intent to do anything on that night other than be a dickhead in front of the boys. That moment of mucking around on the grog cost me the Origin debut I'd hoped and waited so long to have.

In the days and weeks after my sacking, I didn't want to leave the house. I was worried about what the public might say.

I felt like I'd let all the Origin guys down, too. Thankfully, the Blues won the first match of the series 9–8, after Shaun Timmins landed a field goal. I also felt like I'd let down the Dragons' guys because I wasn't going to play for them either. Family and your partner aside, your teammates are the next closest people in your life. I had let them all down, and that's why I really wanted to get back and play.

That opportunity came against the Broncos in Round 12 at Suncorp Stadium – a Friday night blockbuster.

When I ran onto the field, it was to a chorus of boos from the pro-Queensland crowd. It was heavy. Really heavy. It helped when I managed to score a try after just three minutes. I went off during that game with an ankle injury, but came back on after it was needled up and scored another try. But it didn't stop us from losing 24–22.

When the dust had settled after the match, it was revealed that my ankle was bad enough to sideline me for three weeks. What people don't know is that Phil Gould had quietly rung me to see if I was okay to play in Origin II. He wanted me back. The worst thing was my ankle wasn't going to allow it.

This was one of the worst times in my career. Straight after the phone incident, after I was stood down, at least I could train or surf whenever the reality of what had happened came crashing back. That helped to clear my head. But being sidelined through injury puts everything on hold.

From there on, I worked really hard on my rehab, and fortunately enough I came back one game before Origin III, after the Maroons had claimed the second game of the series 22–18 at Suncorp Stadium. I had attempted to come back in Round 15 against the Cowboys, but limped from the field early in the second half because of the ankle problem.

I was pessimistic of my chances of being fit for my Blues debut in the Origin decider, and it would all hinge on the Dragons match against the Wests Tigers at Kogarah Oval.

I was hoping and praying that I was going to get picked for NSW. I knew there were no guarantees because of what had happened, and the simple fact that I hadn't played much football since being sacked. I'd been copping it left, right and centre. I knew one thing, though: I was going to continue to keep my mouth shut. I learnt at that young age that you can't really speak when you've got no credibility. I didn't want to sit there and try to justify myself. I wasn't going to come out publicly and say, 'People don't know me.' I didn't want to come up with that crap. I just wanted to play and get back into what I do. I knew time would heal everything and they'd see what sort of person I am. If you stuff up once, it's a mistake. If you stuff up twice, you've got a problem.

Then the perfect game came out of nowhere. We beat the Tigers 50–0. Trent Barrett had a blinder. And I was lucky enough to score four tries before coming off with the ankle injury.

In the dressing-room, the reporters came looking for me. 'He's had a really hard time in the last month, but he's come through it in the right manner,' Paul McGregor said. 'You can't do much more than score four tries in 60 minutes as far as pushing yourself for the Blues is concerned.'

Then they circled around me. 'I'd be lying if I said I wasn't disappointed when I came off. But I have to manage my ankle, which is not 100 per cent. Everyone would love to play Origin, but at the moment I'm just focused on the Dragons and having fun out there.'

I revisited my push for Origin consideration to *The Sydney Morning Herald* on the eve of selection: 'The only reason people are talking about my form now is what happened three or four weeks ago. It's been a roller-coaster. There probably has been an extra edge [to my form], but that's only because of the circumstances. I think it's a bit hard not to, emotionally and personally, get caught up in it all.'

The following weekend we played Souths on the hallowed turf of the Sydney Cricket Ground, and it was my last chance to impress NSW selectors ahead of Origin III. I was fortunate enough to score another try and set up a couple more, but much of the talk afterwards centered around the fact that Wigan chairman Maurice Lindsay was sitting in the stands.

At the post-match press conference, Nathan Brown said the Dragons would not stand in my way if I wanted to leave – even if I had a year remaining, in 2005, of a three-year deal. He said:

'The last thing we want is Mark leaving, but we gave Gaz an undertaking at the start of the year that if he wants to put in this year to go to England, he can go for a season or two or whatever, as long as when he comes back, he comes back to us. We don't want to be in a situation next February like

Parramatta was with Jamie Lyon. If Jamie Lyon [had played] for Parramatta they would have won at least two more games, but if they knew he wasn't going to be there they could have kept Willie Tonga or bought someone else. The number one result for us is that Gaz stays, but we're going to support whatever he wants to do. At the end of the day, if he goes for a year and then comes back then great, and if he stays [here] that's even better.'

Jamie Lyon had created massive headlines in March that year when he walked out on Parramatta, fled to his home-town of Wee Waa, and asked for a release from the final two years of his contract. It had taken the Eels completely unaware. I was never going to leave the Dragons in the lurch like that.

The sight of Maurice in the Dragons dressing-room after the game caught Browny by surprise. 'It wasn't like he had a suitcase full of cash under each arm, but he knows that I know why he is here,' Browny said, amid media speculation that I was about to be offered a deal worth $2 million to join Wigan.

When I was selected in the NSW side for the decider at the Olympic Stadium, I was ecstatic – and also relieved because I could put the Wigan stuff to the back of my mind. Earning selection for game three was exactly like getting picked again the first time around. Adding to the sweetness of it all was that my Dragons teammates Trent Barrett, Jason Ryles, Brent Kite, Shaun Timmins and Matt Cooper were also named.

Baz was going to play at half-back, with the legend Brad Fittler retained at five-eighth after he had come out of representative retirement for game two following a score of injuries in the halves.

At the medical the next day, the reporters circled me again. This time I was ready to talk.

'It's great to be back,' I said. 'What has happened in the past stays in the past. I've moved on. All I want to do is play football. I want to be part of a NSW side that wins the series.'

Around this same time, news broke that Maurice Lindsay had returned to Australia, and I was again heavily linked to the English powerhouse. I put all that aside. Playing well in my Origin debut, as well as ensuring Freddy Fittler went out a winner in his last match in the sky-blue jumper, was all that mattered.

I also had some people to pay back. My biggest supporter through all of this had been Gus Gould, which might surprise a few people. He had come out in his *Sun-Herald* column a few days after I had been sacked and said he would be quitting Origin for good at the end of this series. People have asked me since if he was filthy – Gus has a reputation for not suffering fools – but he didn't spray me at all. He was pretty understanding, when others weren't.

The best thing Gus did was that he never shut the door on me. I'm certain there would have been enormous pressure from the NSW Rugby League to make sure I didn't play again during that series. Gus went into bat for me and had been in constant contact through the whole ordeal.

He had also pushed for me to come in at right centre ahead of Newcastle's Matt Gidley, who had been a centre I'd really looked up to over the years. That show of faith said to me to forget what's happened and get on with it.

The result was something dreams are made of for a rugby league player, or any professional sportsperson. We won 36–14, and I scored two tries. The first, I just stepped inside and went over. The other one was vintage Freddy, who played down the short side, where I was standing with Willie Mason on the wing. Freddy wrapped me around and, instead of playing short to Mace, played long to me and I scored in the corner.

With 12 minutes to go, after a collision with Benny Ross's elbow, I grabbed the trainer on the field, Ronnie Palmer. 'Oh, I think I've done something to my collarbone,' I said. We were leading comfortably and I was thinking it might be best to have it checked out. 'Maybe I should come off so that I can hopefully play next week for the Saints.'

The message from Gus was pretty clear. 'No way. You'll enjoy this. You're staying until the final whistle.'

And I'm glad I did. I was there when Freddy scored the last try of the match, and there as he sat on my cracked collarbone as we hoisted him from the field.

In the dressing-rooms afterwards I didn't talk to the press, but they were all asking questions about my future and whether I was going to join Wigan on a speculated package of $2 million a year. 'I think he's leaning towards going,' Jason Ryles said.

I didn't have a drink that night because I was trying to get my collarbone right. The next day I had it X-rayed. It showed a crack right through the middle. It wasn't the first or last time I would have broken bones. Me and my chalky bones . . .

It took me about three or four months to have another drink, in public. I was a bit embarrassed to go out, because of people's perceptions. For the next year, fans would make a reference to it when they saw me on the street.

What happened during that Origin series is a part of my life, my history, and I can't avoid it. What I can say is that the Mark Gasnier from 2004 is a lot different to the Mark Gasnier of today.

People have and will make the assumption that I had a problem with alcohol. I didn't. I would drink like every other player: socially and when we had a chance. If we'd played a Friday night game and had Saturday and Sunday off, then we would have a beer.

Did I have a problem? Definitely not. I sometimes didn't know when to go home, but there was never a moment when I thought: *God, I've got to get off the grog.*

If anything, you wouldn't have a beer for two months and then you'd have an all-nighter. Footy players epitomise binge drinking, to a certain extent. Because we have a limited opportunity to go out, when we do have the opportunity we make the most of it.

When I met my future wife, Claudine, a few years after that Origin series, she knew about the incident. When we first started going out, she mentioned my name to her brother-in-law because she didn't know anything about football. 'Oh, that's the one who did the phone call,' he said. Her response to me sums up why I love her: 'Well, you know, this is what you did. It's none of my business.'

Claude and I we grew really close straightaway, and I'd like to think after a few months she saw what sort of a person I really am. She saw my family, she saw what morals and ethics I have. And to be honest, I was a lot more mature when I met Claude.

Now that we've got a little boy, I realise that you just can't do anything that reflects poorly on you as a person, because you represent a lot more than yourself. You represent your family.

So I'll cop it for what I did. I am truly sorry. The biggest message that came from it all was that challenges in life make you grow up. You learn from it. If it's the worst thing I ever do, then I'll be happy.

Did I ever speak to the girl from that night? I called her number and apologised. I left a message, oddly enough, but a message of a very different kind: 'I'm really sorry, that just isn't me.'

SEVEN

'WHY WOULD YOU LEAVE THIS?'

A CHINESE RESTAURANT IS the place where many deals have been done over the years, especially in rugby league. The Golden Century at Fox Studios in Moore Park, Sydney, is the place where Peter Doust convinced me that I shouldn't walk away from the game.

Which was a good thing, because in my mind I had already gone.

Jason Ryles was right when he said after that epic win for New South Wales against Queensland that I was leaning towards going. I was certainly heading that way.

As I've explained, there was interest in late 2003, and there was more interest at the start of 2004 when I was supposedly disillusioned with the game, about signing with Wigan. But this time, after the dramas of the Origin series, I was definitely ready to go.

★

'I wouldn't dream of negotiating a contract with anybody who has got a State of Origin match to come,' Maurice had told the press. 'You can rest assured that I won't be interfering with anybody's mental state before a vital game. I can assure you there is no contract signed between me and Mark, or indeed anybody else at this stage.'

That's not entirely right. Nothing had been signed, but we had met. My manager, George, and I met the Wigan boss at the famous Catalina restaurant at Rose Bay. He explained that he wanted me. The money was good – about $2.5 million over four years. But it wasn't so much the perks of going as the thought of no longer being in Australia and the National Rugby League that appealed more. It was an easy way out from all that had been swirling around me.

People often think that player managers use interest from other clubs or competing interests to leverage a new contract or a new deal with the existing club or sponsor. That wasn't the case at all. I had two seasons – until the end of 2006 – to run on my deal with the Dragons. George wasn't pushing me to go. He was just doing his job, because I was seriously thinking of going.

After the Origin victory in game three, Peter Doust asked me, 'Gaz, why would you want to leave all this?'

It was a fair enough question. The truth? I was fucked off.

I was copping that much flak – and a $50,000 fine to go with it. The media and the public had their different opinions, and they tried to cut it at every angle that suited them. At one point, I even started to think that I wasn't entirely to blame. My head was all over the place. *Maybe someone from management shouldn't have put me in that position to drink that many beers . . .* Well, that's bullshit. At the end of the day I did it. It's my problem. I have to wear it.

There was intense media interest surrounding my next destination, and it was being played out in the papers every day. The Dragons is a club that will always have salary cap issues because of the quality of the juniors they can produce. They had already seen our popular hooker Mark Riddell sign with Parramatta. Prop Brent Kite had done a big deal to go to the Sea Eagles. Half-back Brett Firman was headed for the Roosters.

The club had made it clear to me in March that I would be released if I wanted to, as Nathan Brown had said after the Souths game on the eve of Origin III. But if I went it would be with strict conditions. 'We certainly wouldn't want him playing in the NRL against us,' Dousty had said. 'And I'd be looking for terms that he not be allowed to play for any other NRL club if we were to release him. Their line of thinking was that if I did go for a year, and got away from everything that had been happening in Sydney, I could possibly return to the Dragons. The Wigan offer was for four years, but it had a get-out clause at the end of every year.

At the end of our meal, I'd all but told Maurice that I would join Wigan from 2005 onwards. I had been speaking to Peter throughout the process, and I told him that I would be wanting that release. When the time came to collect the release form, we met at the Golden Century. He pulled it out, all filled in, with the exception of his signature to make it official. 'Gaz,' he said. 'If I sign this release form and let you go,

I will be doing an injustice by the team, by the club . . . and by you.'

That was the moment when I knew I didn't want to go. I had too much left to do in the game. I realised that I had to front up to what I had done, not run away. I was being an immature sook by not staying. So I changed my mind.

I phoned Maurice and told him my final decision. He wasn't very happy, but most of his anger was directed at Peter Doust, who had indicated all along that I could gain a release if I wanted it.

After I signed, Maurice told *Rugby League Week*, 'While I was in Australia, I had the opportunity to sign Ryan Cross before he agreed to stay at the Roosters. At that time, I was again assured by Mark's agency that the deal would happen. I left a contract with them, which I had signed, when I left. Everyone in Sydney knew the club was prepared to release him and we got that confirmed formally from his managers. Over three days, we agreed to terms with Darryl Mather [George Mimis's business partner] from SFX management . . . and today I received a call from Mark saying the club had refused to release him.'

Dousty responded in the *Sun-Herald* by saying, 'Maurice didn't get his man and that doesn't happen very often to Wigan. Maurice isn't used to it and he's embarrassed, so he's trying to save face. I like Maurice and I enjoy doing business with him, but on this occasion we couldn't do business and that didn't suit him. He had an expectation that he was going to be able to get Mark and it didn't happen.'

I want to acknowledge now that Peter Doust took a bullet

to protect me publicly and made himself look like the bad guy. He took all the blame. Maurice Lindsay will probably read this and think: *You bastard.* But that's the truth. Peter Doust had never said he wouldn't release me, I was the one who said I didn't want to go.

The worst part about it all was that I did not get back on the field that season. The broken collarbone was supposed to lay me low for about three weeks, but then I re-fractured it while pulling myself out of a car in Jason Ryles's garage.

But that's not the end of it. Later that week, Trent Barrett and I were driving to Wollongong to meet the team bus before heading to the airport to fly out for the game against North Queensland and we had an accident. We ran up the back of the car in front while my arm was in a sling. Baz's four-wheel drive was a mess.

That was the year when the wolves really starting crying for Nathan Brown's head. We finished fifth by the end of the season, but then we lost to Penrith 31–30 in the first game of the play-offs. After North Queensland beat the Bulldogs and Melbourne defeated the Broncos in the first weekend of the finals, we were buried after the first week because of the McIntyre System.

Naturally, the calls for Nathan Brown's head started straightaway.

My own worries continued. During the following off-season, every time I tried to put my seatbelt on, my wrist kept popping out of the joint. I was told that I needed a wrist reconstruction and would miss the first month of the next season. Great – my luck continued.

Yet, despite all of these setbacks, I wanted to go on. I grew up a lot that season, because I wanted to walk away to Wigan over something that was stupid, and I realised it would be a bad mistake.

You should be man enough to say, 'Mate – guilty. I'm sorry, I've got to get on with it. I'll cop whatever I get.' Nobody put the beer in my hand, and if they did I didn't have to drink it. I think that's where my lack of maturity came into it – I was looking for a way out. I am more than happy to write, here and now, that I handled that whole transfer situation poorly. I was trying to run away from a situation that I had created through my own mistake. If it had happened to me later in my career, I'd have handled it a lot differently.

EIGHT

THE CHOKE

I'D PLAYED FOR STATE and country, had experienced plenty of highs and lows, but on the eve of the 2005 season I felt I had accomplished nothing. This might sound strange, but it was how I was feeling about my game and career at the time.

I'd played 75 matches over five seasons, and the injury and dramas of the previous season didn't allow me to play consistent football – or train, for that matter. Until then, the 2001 season had been the only time when I had managed to string together consistent games, and by that I mean 80 minutes, week in, week out. I wanted a lot more out of the game.

A lot of people who knew football would say to me, 'We'd love to see you play nine or ten games in a row.' That comment never cut me up – I never worried about the outside world too much – but they made a valid point: I barely got to play more than four games straight and had not realised my potential. It was nothing I didn't already know.

Ask anyone in the league and they will tell you that playing consistent football gives you a lot of confidence. You get into that weekly groove, that routine. You are preparing as you should. Up until that point, I had felt comfortable in my own skin. I felt confident among my teammates and that I could certainly mix it up at this level. I belonged here. But the time had come to please myself more than anyone else and play to a level *I* felt content with, because self-satisfaction is the best feeling you can get after a game, knowing you've played to your potential and haven't let anyone down. I never told anyone, but I had made it very clear in my mind that 2005 would be the season when I proved to myself as much as anyone what I was capable of as a footballer.

This was also the season when it was time for the Dragons to realise their potential as a group. The expectation on Nathan Brown and Peter Doust – all of us – to finally win a premiership was gathering momentum. The noise had always been there, but it was getting louder. On the eve of the historic Charity Shield match against South Sydney, Browny went so far as to say that this was a make-or-break year for him as a coach: 'One bad year can lead to not having a job.'

Browny was already under pressure. At the start of every season he was being flogged in the press. Finishing fifth the previous season and failing to go past Penrith in the first week of the finals series fuelled the frustration. Losing the first four out of five games didn't help either.

That was the *outside* perception. Personally, I didn't think he was a chance of losing his job. I would speak to the officials and I never heard one of them mention a bad word about the coach. Dousty always backed Browny – he was his biggest supporter. The Dragons board was really solid as well. Those directors, even now, are very understanding people. They don't try to create the pressure-cooker environment you often see at other clubs, especially when things are going poorly. And that isn't an easy thing to do, I imagine, given the weight of history at the club.

I think Browny knew that he had everyone's backing, even though I reckon the media – or some sections of it – had an agenda against the club and Dousty. You get that scrutiny at any club, but we seemed to cop a little bit more because of who we are. The Dragons are one of the most popular teams in the game. We had high-profile players at the time. On the other side of the equation, you get extra sponsorship, praise and reward when things are going well. It's a situation a lot of us young people at the time didn't always accept: with greater hype, profile and money comes a hell of a lot of responsibility and expectation. Younger players these days have to understand that if you want all the trappings of being a high-profile footballer, you have to expect to be in the spotlight and accountable 24/7. Only when I became a bit older and wiser did I realise that life at the club cut both ways.

Shaun Timmins gave an insight into life under the magnifying glass on the eve of the season in an interview with *The Daily Telegraph*: 'We finished fifth last season. There were ten other sides behind us, but they don't seem to cop the same crap from fans and the media as we do. People do expect more of us because of our tradition and history. That adds pressure, I suppose, but we expect it and try not to let it worry us.'

By 2005 we had a core group of blokes who had been together for some years – for some of us, throughout our entire first-grade careers. Players like myself, Jason Ryles, Luke Bailey, Matty Cooper and Ben Hornby. Then we had players like Trent Barrett, Shaun Timmins and Lance Thompson, who had been there before us. We had the nucleus to win it all, so the expectation was fair enough, although I don't think fans and critics realise just how hard it is to actually do it.

Personally, I never felt better. Despite the wrist injury I suffered in Trent Barrett's car in late November and the subsequent reconstructive surgery, I was only going to miss the first four rounds. I was in the best headspace I had been in for much of my career, so it didn't get to me as much as the previous injuries.

In 2001, when I wasn't suffering any injuries and could get into my routine, I would retreat to my second-favourite sporting love and work in a surf. Then, in 2002 and 2003, I got away from surfing because I was injured all the time and thought I would have to concentrate on my rehab. I didn't think I could do both and somehow intertwine them so that my body would be fresh and ready to go on game day.

Something Phil Gould had said to me during the Origin series really helped. When Gus gives you frank advice, as he tends to do, you are best to listen.

'Gaz, I don't know you,' he began. 'But watching you from

afar, you need balance in your life. Balance things out. Don't think you're doing the wrong thing by your football career if you want to go surfing and get away from football. When you're not training, go do it.'

He assured me that I wouldn't be doing my football an injustice by surfing. It didn't mean I didn't care. In fact, it would keep me fresh. I realised that keeping my mind clear and not always thinking about footy was brilliant advice that would serve me well for the rest of the year.

Unfortunately, all of the positive signs didn't translate into a very good start to the season for the Dragons. Heavy losses to the Bulldogs and Melbourne, then another two defeats to Penrith and Canberra meant that we were winless and dead last on the ladder heading into the Round 5 match against Manly at Wollongong. We won that one. 'Stop the presses – Saints win a game' was one of the more memorable headlines, and typical of those over the last two years.

Right on cue, the pressure on Browny started to mount because of our slow start. The rumour mill cranked up about Timmo and the coach having a fall out, something Timmo came out publicly to deny, as so many of us had to do when speculation got out of control. Without making excuses, injury had played a big part in how things had been going. A stat came out before our game against Brisbane: not since May 2003 had Baz, Timmo, Cooper, Ryles, Bailey and I played together in the one match.

The media can also swing the other way. After we beat the Tigers, a game in which I had a pretty strong performance, they were declaring that we had bounced back and 'breathed fire' into our season. But from there we suffered from more indifferent form over the next few weeks. If not for a side-line conversion after the full-time siren from half-back Matt Head against the Roosters in the Anzac Day clash at the SFS, we would've been really struggling.

The representative season always hurts the Dragons because so many of our players earn selection. Heading into the 2005 State of Origin series, the same was about to happen, even if we were still outside the top eight. The last thing any of us were thinking was that we were in a position to win the 2005 premiership so many people expected of us.

After what I went through in the lead-up to Origin 2004, the last thing you would've thought I wanted to get involved in was a bonding session before the first game of the 2005 series. It was on my mind, but the night turned out to be one of the best of my career.

Our new coach for this series was Ricky Stuart, the Roosters coach who had won a premiership in his first season on the job in 2003. Phil Gould had made it clear, after the phone call incident the year before, that he wouldn't be continuing in the job. As a proud New South Welshman who had led the Blues to Origin series victories as a player from half-back, 'Stick' was a perfect replacement.

I hadn't had a coach at that stage quite like Ricky. Gus was a tactical coach in many ways, whereas Ricky just showed pure emotion. Some coaches can fake that type of passion, but it didn't take us very long to know he wasn't bullshitting. You can't bullshit that consistently. He was genuinely passionate about Origin, and he loved New South Wales.

I appreciated his whole approach for that series and the way he brought all former players who had worn the sky-blue jumper back into the fold. And that's how I found myself, on the first bonding night of the session at the Charing Cross Hotel, having a drink with Steve Rogers, the original Prince of Centres, better known as 'Sludge'. And only as Sludge would have it, we were drinking red wine at a rapid rate.

It wasn't supposed to happen like that, but halfway through the night the backs and the forwards had teamed up with players in their positions from the past. Over in one corner, Steve 'Blocker' Roach was holding court with the forwards. Matty King, the Melbourne Storm winger who would be outside me on the field, was in another corner with Sludge and me. It reflected a great level of respect between current and past players, and the positions they shared.

I knew how good Steve Rogers was during his career with the Dragons and Cronulla. A lot of people said to me he was the best centre they had ever seen, after Uncle Reg. Because I knew the high regard Reg was held in by the football community, I knew how much that must have meant.

I'd seen video footage of Sludge, and knew the way he stepped – actually, it was more like a swerve. His son, Mat, was almost identical in the way he moved, like a Ducati going around a hairpin corner, an arc at pace.

All we did was talk about football. It was funny – I was so

interested in his era, but he was so interested in mine. Sludge talked about the game back in his day – the pace, the timing – and wanted to know how it was for us.

People say the bonding session shouldn't be allowed, and maybe after what had happened in 2004 I should be the last one defending it, but I have to say that night with Steve Rogers was unforgettable. In January the following year, at the age of 51, Sludge passed away after swallowing a combination of prescription drugs and alcohol. The coroner said it was an accident, not suicide as many had speculated. It was devastating, and makes that night I shared with him even more special.

As I approached the 2005 series, I was very focused. After the dramas and injuries that had set me back over the early years of my career, I was itching for the chance to play a full Origin series for New South Wales.

Like almost every Origin match, the build-up to game one at Suncorp Stadium in Brisbane was intense, and more so when Ricky and Queensland counterpart Michael Hagan started trading barbs in the media about tactics. Hagan complained that we would use so-called wrestling techniques, while Ricky hit back and said he was expecting the Maroons to 'surrender' in tackles, hoping to give their little men a quick play-the-ball. Ricky saw it as an attempt from Queensland to pressure referee Paul Simpkins.

That stuff happens with Origin. There's so much hype and talk and speculation, and you have to do your best to block it out. At the end of the day, you know the role you have to play and the task at hand. And it's also the last thing you think about when you are trailing 19–0 after 50 minutes in front of a massive crowd of 52,000 Queenslanders.

Somehow, we clawed our way back into the game, bridging the gap to 19–14 with 10 minutes to play. Trent Barrett and I managed to combine well on the short-side down the right, putting Matty King away down the touchline. Just as Maroons full-back Billy Slater converged, Matty hurled the ball in field and hooker Danny Buderus scored. It was our fourth try in 18 minutes.

Backrower Craig Fitzgibbon kicked the conversion and we were ahead 20–19 – somehow – and seemingly headed for one of those great Origin comeback victories, before Maroons half-back Johnathan Thurston landed a field goal with two minutes remaining to send the match into golden-point extra time.

Then came the moment that will go down in Origin folklore. Half-back Brett Kimmorley had been in great form for the Sharks. 'Noddy' had been the player who had kept Andrew Johns out of rep sides in the past, but he earned selection for this match because Joey had been sidelined for weeks with a broken jaw. Noddy was a very damaging half-back when sides used sliding defence. It was actually Ricky's up-and-in defence, which he started using during his early coaching days at the Roosters, that ruined playmakers like Noddy, who would run to the defensive line and put his outside men into gaps.

It also made them susceptible to throwing intercept passes, and so it was that three minutes into golden point Noddy, having numbers and space on the left side of the field, drifted across and threw a long cut-out pass, trying to find Matty Cooper. Instead, it found Maroons replacement Matt Bowen, who raced away to score the match-winner.

It was a devastating way to lose a game, and the calls for change for the must-win return game in Sydney started almost as soon as the final whistle sounded. Ricky had made it clear in the post-match press conference, as he had to us in the dressing-rooms afterwards, that he wanted to keep the same blokes for game two. But then, after the round of footy that weekend, he made it clear at a luncheon that he might reconsider.

'I did say I was happy to go with the same 18 players, but to be quite honest, after what some of our players dished up on the weekend for our club teams, you can only ask for so much loyalty or ask selectors to show loyalty,' Ricky said when interviewed on stage. 'The selectors are there to do a job, and we're all there to win a game of football. And if there's got to be changes made, well, I can understand what the selectors are thinking.'

I was fortunate enough to be selected, especially since we would be playing with Andrew Johns, who had made himself available after coming back from his broken jaw just 10 days before Origin II. Joey had thrown an intercept pass in his return match against Brisbane, in addition to being penalised for a high tackle and failing to stop the Knights from losing their eleventh match in a row. 'I'm a certainty,' he had laughed when asked if he should be picked. But they picked him anyway, because if anyone deserved to be selected on reputation alone it was Andrew Johns.

The very first ball-work session of that camp was at Woollahra Oval in Sydney's eastern suburbs, and the rest of us knew straightaway, from the moment Joey appeared, how special this was going to be.

A lot of people think of Joey as the player with freakish skills, an unbelievable reader of the game, an unbelievable ball player – and he is all of that – but what they don't see is that he's just as passionate as blokes like Sticky when it comes to the NSW jumper. He just doesn't show it as much. From that very first session the entire team lifted around him because we could see how much it meant to him. He set the standard.

Everything just flowed, everything was sharp. I'm not being disrespectful to Noddy, but Joey was focused and adamant right from the start that he wanted to win that series – and we felt it, too. It was like he was suddenly coaching the team alongside Ricky, even if he hadn't been a part of the preparation until this day. At the end of the session we all looked at each other and said, 'How good is this?'

Behind the scenes, however, Joey was actually very nervous about his comeback. He was returning from a broken jaw, but the previous year had been all but wiped out with a knee reconstruction. For most players, it takes 18 months for a full recovery.

He was putting his balls on the line. Everything he had done, his entire reputation, and he was coming back late in his career into a side that had lost the first game and was staring down an Origin series defeat. We were up against history: in 25 years, only one Blues side had come back from losing the first game to claim the series.

Much of the media talk directed at me throughout the series had been about how I felt in relation to the *last* series. 'That's in the past. It's irrelevant,' was the comment I kept repeating. What else could I say? I was just excited about the next two games with Joey back. Then I felt a twinge in my groin late in the week, and all of a sudden I was in serious doubt . . . again. In the end, I was allowed up until the day before the game to pass a fitness test – beating Luke Lewis in a sprint – and I did.

'I'm 100 per cent and can't wait to get out there and help New South Wales to victory,' I told *The Daily Telegraph*. 'I'm relieved and now very excited I'll be playing. It's one of the biggest matches of my career and I won't let anyone down. I want to thank Ricky for giving me the chance to prove I'm fit and the medical team for getting me on the field.'

Game day. I had never felt anything like it. Game three last year, when I had come back and been a part of Brad Fittler's last rep match, was one thing. This was something else. There were 82,000 fans at Stadium Australia at Homebush, almost all of them wanting a Blues victory.

My night changed dramatically late in the first half when Luke Rooney on the left wing suffered an adductor injury. That meant I was suddenly switched from right centre into his vacant position on the left wing, playing outside of my Dragons teammate Matt Cooper. The Maroons led 12–8 at half-time, but then Joey turned on a performance that will go down in history as one of the greatest ever played in Origin – definitely the best from a player to wear the sky-blue jumper.

His passing and running games were superb, but not as much as his kicking game, which had been instrumental in all five NSW tries. But it was also his vision – he threw a beautiful cut-out pass that hit me on the chest on our 30-metre line, and I raced downfield before getting the pass inside for Coops to score. We won 32–22 and, with the series all squared up, Ricky spoke for all of us when he said of Joey on Channel Nine, 'I have never seen a player come to a training session and lift them by 25 per cent.'

When you are out there on the paddock, you are not as aware as the public of another individual's performance. You can gauge *effort* a lot better, but close to 16 cameras sees a lot more detail! As a player you're caught up in the moment. It's just happening. You're concentrating on your own game. We were so happy to win and everyone was getting on board with the task at hand. It's not until I watched the replay later that I realised how dominant Joey had been.

In the decider in Brisbane, Joey did it again. He took complete control, although it was the opening period of the match, when we defended our line for seven sets in a row – 29 tackles – that set it up. That's when we knew we had a close-knit team, and when Mini at full-back scooped up a grubber kick and ran 90 metres to score, we were away. When Ricky coached NSW in 2011, he showed us video of that period, to show what Origin was about.

We ended up leading 18–0 at half-time and eventually won 32–10. It was Queensland's heaviest defeat in front of their home crowd, and the first time since 1994 that the Blues had come back from a game down to win the series. It was our third series victory in a row and, while we all played a big part and had become so tight, it is only with time that I can appreciate what Joey did. Only now do I realise how much he put himself out there. A lot of players would just rest on their laurels, but he risked it all.

People often ask me if he was the best I'd played alongside, and in terms of all-round ability I would have to say he was, for his ball-playing, his vision, the influence he had on the game. He was a great defender, a great attacker, a great talker, a great thinker, but above all he was a fierce competitor. I think of players in terms of their individual positions, and I think of Knights centre Matt Gidley. He had some of the best footwork I'd seen. But in terms of an all-round game, there was none better than Joey. He will always be the benchmark.

I hear how good some halves are these days – and there are some very, very good ones out there – but I think there is a general lack of halves in recent seasons compared to when Joey first started, to other periods in the 1980s and 1990s when it was impossible to work out who should be the Australian half-back.

In my opinion, none of them are as good as Andrew Johns.

While I had experienced two of the greatest highs of my career playing for New South Wales, the expectation continued to build around us at St George Illawarra. We had become a very solid and consistent footy team. We quickly overcame the fact that we had players scattered throughout the Blues side, and as the home-and-away season started to gather momentum we were playing as well as we ever had.

Before the local derby against Cronulla at Kogarah Oval, their backrower Paul Gallen had said we weren't tough enough mentally to win a comp. We knew that was rubbish. We knew we were tough enough, and we ended up beating them that afternoon. I had helped with a pass to the winger outside of me on the right edge, Colin Best, who scored a decisive try just before half-time. As I've mentioned, a lot of it comes down to instinct. 'You can't practise it, touch wood,' I said to the reporters after the game. 'It's not something you're conscious of. It just happens, the way the game goes, and fortunately it came off.'

The most important words were said by Browny in the dressing-room that afternoon. 'You can't take it for granted, what we've got at the moment,' he said. 'We might not be together again in a couple of years' time. It's very important to make the most of the talent we've got.'

He was right. At the end of 2006 we had a lot of players coming off contract, blokes like Trent Barrett, Lance Thompson and Shaun Timmins. Matt Cooper, who was playing as well as anyone in the game, was also coming off contract – and so was I. Browny had been a part of losing three Grand Finals. He knew that the planets don't align that often, and they seemed to be aligning for us.

A week after the victory over the Sharks, I managed to score three tries against the Ricky Stuart-coached Roosters.

Having coached me at Origin level, he reckoned I'd never been in better form. I was just happy to be contributing.

Browny spoke to reporters after the game. 'I never saw his uncle Reg play, so I can't really comment on that [comparison]. [Mark's] obviously a wonderful player. Gaz is a much better player now because he has been through some tough times with injury and last year with the Origin thing. He's matured as a person and now he's actually one of the leaders of the side. Gaz will tell you himself that frame of mind wasn't a part of him. He was a naturally talented young kid, and now he's grown into a man. The game doesn't have to come to him. If the team's in trouble, Gaz will go to the game.'

I'd lived with the comparisons with Uncle Reg for as long as I could remember – which I'll address later – but I look back now and think I was playing consistently because I wasn't injured. I definitely didn't look after my body back then like I did later in my career, but I was revelling in the fact that I was on the park for a change. I felt like I was making up for lost time and trying to realise my potential, just as I had set out to do at the start of the season.

The more matches we won as the finals approached, the more critics and so-called 'experts' started bringing out a word that we had heard before: chokers. We had heard it at the start of the year when we lost four in a row; we were hearing it now. Before the match against the Broncos – probably our biggest test to date because they were leading the comp – Browny was asked if we had peaked too early.

'Everyone used to say we were inconsistent, and now that we're winning they're looking for another excuse. Sides that

Me at nine months old.

My first photo with Santa. As you can see, fashion has changed a bit!

Getting our individual photos for Renown United under-10s. If only I had that much hair now.

My seventh birthday, wearing my beloved Woodger's Canberra jersey. It had the number 7 on the back, since I was a big Ricky Stuart fan as a kid.

A proud moment, receiving the under-9s grand final Man of the Match off Steve Linnane at Kogarah Oval.

An action shot from the under-9s grand final with the original Kogarah Oval in the background.

Runners-up at the state carnival, we were very disappointed since we had gone through undefeated in every other competition that year.

Under-11s grand final, again at Kogarah Oval. We had won the under-9s and under-10s and were going for our third straight grand final victory, which we ended up winning against Hurstville United.

Metropolitan under-15s representative team. (*Middle row, fourth in from the right*) As you can see, I'm going through a bit of a surfer stage with the hair!

Good times. My first-grade debut up at Marathon Stadium against the Knights in 2000. (Photo: Carlos Furtado/Action Photographics)

I was very fortunate to launch the Kids to Kangaroos program in 2002 after debuting for my country in 2001. I'm with Uncle Reg and my little cousin, Jack. (Photo: Brett Costello/Newspix)

Regrettable times, fronting the media scrum outside the St George Leagues Club following the infamous phone call incident in 2004. (Photo: Erica Harrison/ Newspix)

Happier times, making my debut for NSW in 2004. I scored two tries and won my first Origin series. (Photos: Robb Cox/Action Photographics)

One of the best moments of my career, winning Origin III in Queensland in 2005. I played all three games in the series. (Photo: Charles Knight/Action Photographics)

Even though we suffered a heart-breaking loss to Wests in the 2005 preliminary finals, I had a great day against the Tigers in 2004 at Kogarah Oval, scoring four tries and getting a Perfect 10 from *Rugby League Week*. (Photo: Jonathan Ng/Action Photographics)

Getting sprung by the media after meeting some people from the ARU at my manager George's office in 2006. (Photo: Noel Kessel/ Newspix)

I don't remember much about this photo, after getting knocked out cold from a high shot by Steve Matai during a 2008 Test in Wellington against New Zealand. (Photo: Brett Costello/ Newspix)

Kicking the ball in the 2007 Charity Shield match against South Sydney after being shifted to five-eighth, only to go on to tear my pectoral muscle and miss 19 weeks. (Photo: Jonathan Ng/Action Photographics)

Getting some attention after splitting my eye and hurting my cheekbone, having returned from my pec tear in the latter parts of 2007. (Photo: Robb Cox/Action Photographics)

It was one of the proudest moments of my career when I was named the sole captain of the Dragons in 2008, only to be forced into announcing my move to Stade Francais at a press conference in July of that year. (Photo: Sam Mooy/Newspix)

What I thought would be my last hurrah, losing to Manly in the first semifinal of 2008 at Brookvale. (Photo: Gregg Porteous/Newspix)

Rugby, Top 14/Stade Français

« J'adore déjà Paris »

MARK GASNIER, nouveau trois-quarts australien du Stade Français

Gasnier, star anonyme

Big Red V to pretty in pink for Gaz

A sample of some of the headlines I made in France and at home. Basically, they're saying that I love Paris already and am the 'anonymous star'.

I'm standing in front of the Arc de Triomphe, for those of you who aren't familiar with Paris, for the French sports paper *L'Equipe*.

Making my debut for Stade Francais in the Top 14 against Bourgoin at Grenoble. (Photo: Ross Hodgson/Newspix)

Just showing off one of my favourite jerseys! (Photo: Lionel Bonaventure/AFP/Getty Images)

The amazing atmosphere at Stade de France, one of six games a year we would play at that exciting venue.

Touching down for the first try in the 2010 Grand Final after a perfect Jamie Soward kick. (Photo: Grant Trouville/Action Photographics)

The ultimate prize and greatest feeling in a footballer's career: holding the NRL Premiership trophy aloft. It was fantastic to share it with that bloke next to me: Benny Hornby. (Photo: Grant Trouville/ Action Photographics)

I was very happy to run out for the Blues again in 2011 after my two-year stint in France. (Photo: Grant Trouville/Action Photographics)

My last game at a ground that meant so much to me, Kogarah Oval – or WIN Jubilee Oval, as it is now known. (Photo: Renee McKay/Action Photographics)

Claude and me hiding from the weather for a photo opportunity.

Our pride and joy, Kalani.

My most treasured hobby: surfing. (Photo: Blue Snapper)

win the minor premiership, no one ever says they peak too soon. If we beat the Broncos, they'll look for another reason why we're going to lose. Everyone just looks for reasons why we should win and, now we're winning, they're looking for reasons why we should get beat.' I echoed his thoughts in a separate interview: 'Some people are waiting for us to start losing.'

Then we beat the Broncos in front of a big crowd at Suncorp Stadium.

Two weeks later, the game against Parramatta at Kogarah Oval was being billed as 'the match of the year'. The pressure was building. We beat them 25–23 in a blockbuster and the bookies installed us as premiership favourites. Before the final-round match against the Knights, their coach, Michael Hagan, doubted how well we could perform in the finals, saying, 'I still think maybe the jury is still out on their ability to win big games, semifinal games, and whether they're going to be good enough to go all the way.'

Again, he was entitled to his opinion . . . Then we beat Newcastle and finished the regular season on the same amount of points as Parramatta, but they were crowned minor premiers because of a better for-and-against differential. In the first final, against Cronulla at WIN Stadium in Wollongong, we won but won ugly. We knew we had to improve, but because we were one of the highest ranked teams to win, we progressed to the preliminary final and had a week off.

We were within one game of the Grand Final, but who would our opponents be? The Wests Tigers were playing the same attacking football that we were, and after pumping the Cowboys the first week of the finals, they advanced after defeating Brisbane. So it was decided: Dragons vs. Tigers at the Sydney Football Stadium for the right to play in the Grand Final.

We were installed as short-price favourites and expected to go through and meet Parramatta, according to the press. We had a really good preparation in the lead-up to the game; we went into camp two days before the match and trained really well. We were excited, everything was pointing to a good performance.

But what we dished up was quite the opposite.

The simple fact is we didn't perform anywhere near the level we could have or should have. We capitulated. We dropped the ball. We gave away too many penalties. We had left it to the most important hour to bring out our worst game of the season. Maybe you could put it down to the fact that none of us – or not many of us – had been in such a strong position to win a comp before. But the Tigers were in the same boat. And knowing what I know now, we choked that game.

Afterwards, nobody said a word in the sheds. We just sat there. It's not the fact that we lost that was on our minds – everyone knew what had happened – it's the *way* we had lost. You're always disappointed in the wake of defeat, but when you play as poorly as we did on an occasion like that, it's magnified dramatically. We had blown a big opportunity.

Of all the disappointments I've had playing for the Dragons, none hurt as much as that one. Until that point, it was the saddest moment of my career.

NINE

NOW OR NEVER

THE DUST WAS ONLY just starting to settle on our preliminary final loss to the Wests Tigers when a new issue came up. Actually, it was the very next morning after the game.

WALLABIES BOMBSHELL: WE WANT GASNIER blared the headline in *The Sunday Telegraph*, indicating that the Australian Rugby Union wanted to sign me on a $2 million deal with the 2007 World Cup in France in mind. The 15-man code had already lured Lote Tuqiri, Mat Rogers and Wendell Sailor away from rugby league, and now – according to this story – they were after me. 'If he became available we'd certainly be interested in him,' Wallabies then-coach Eddie Jones said in the story.

That's when the typical paper talk that happens around this sort of situation cranked up, even though I was contracted to the Dragons until the end of the 2006 season.

Then the ARU came out a day later and said they weren't interested.

I commented a week after the first story appeared, ahead of the Tri Nations tour of England: 'If Eddie wants to talk to me after the Tri Nations, I'm more than happy to talk to him. Union is something I'm not ruling out, but the way I feel is they would have to be fair dinkum about it. I don't know how interested they are. But if they are keen, I'm prepared to have a chat.'

The truth is I had never seen myself playing another code. I had never seen myself playing for a club other than St George Illawarra, for that matter. As I would learn later in my career, you should never say never.

Things were coming to a head at the Dragons. I wasn't the only one coming off contract. Trent Barrett, Shaun Timmins, Matt Cooper, Ben Creagh, Mathew Head, Justin Poore, Ashton Sims and Dean Young – 13 players in total – were all being circled by rival clubs.

That was due to the nature of the salary cap and the club's history of producing and nurturing so many talented players – as it does today and will into the future. Something had to give. We also knew the upcoming 2006 season would be the end of an era either way. In terms of a potential premiership, people were already saying it: now or never.

Broncos great Darren Lockyer said it was ours to win and installed us as pre-season favourites. Baz fronted the crowd at our season launch: 'We can't keep waiting for next year. We have to make the most of *this* year.'

Despite what others were saying, I don't think we had a

'now-or-never' mentality, but there was little doubt the stars were starting to align. I didn't read too much into it. I had enough on my mind. We all did.

From early January and well into the season, Trent was linked to a big offer with Wigan, just as I had been in the past, and there was a get-out clause in his contract that allowed him to go if he wanted to. There were discussions behind the scenes that if Trent left I would be moved to five-eighth, but it was all speculation.

The starting point for me, like every contract negotiation I ever had with St George Illawarra, was that I did not want to go anywhere else. I can pretty much say every player at that club, at that time, would have been prepared to take less to stay. I received bigger offers to go elsewhere in 2001, but I stayed because I loved the Dragons.

My way of thinking, which I conveyed to my manager, George, was that if the Saints were always prepared to pay me my market value, I wouldn't even look elsewhere. If you're happy to receive what you think you're worth, and the club is prepared to pay it, you don't look outside the square, unlike in rugby union.

When the ARU learnt that I wasn't prepared to quickly dismiss them, I found myself meeting new Wallabies coach, John Connolly, and dual-international Michael O'Connor in George's offices in the city.

It was a great meeting, like having a beer with a couple of people I'd known for years. Michael O'Connor made a lot of sense when he spoke – so did John Connolly. They simply explained what rugby was about. It wasn't so much the money that was rugby union's selling point, although that was a part of it, it was the game's global appeal. It was truly international. 'The money's not the issue,' John said. 'You can only go and play Leichhardt Oval so many times before you want a change.'

He asked me what I liked doing, what appealed to me outside of football, and one of the things I mentioned was travelling. That became John's big selling point: rugby would provide me an opportunity to travel all over the world. Then they asked what my views on rugby were, and I said I felt I wouldn't touch the ball if I crossed codes, but John was confident that I could make a 'seamless transition'.

When I look back now, I can say that when I eventually went to French rugby I didn't have the drive to play for the national team like I did in league. I wasn't as ambitious over there, which I guess proves you have to love the sport to be driven to succeed.

But if I had gone to rugby in 2007, as they were asking, if I was going to make a proper fist of it, I would have played Super Rugby and tried to play for Australia in the World Cup. At the time, Matty Giteau was playing five-eighth, and he was on fire. I felt like I probably would get a bit of ball off him. John Connolly assured me that they planned on throwing it around under his coaching.

I wasn't convinced that I could make a 'seamless transition'. What makes a good player a great player is their instinctive play and the things that come naturally on the football field. And I always knew that rugby would never come naturally to me. Yes, I could've utilised my skills and done some good things here and there, but instinct is what made me play rugby league well. I don't think I would have had that in rugby. I could never become a champion.

That meeting was one of several. I met with Matty Rogers, who was now at the NSW Waratahs, and coach Ewen McKenzie. Mat had written an open letter in the paper saying, 'Come to rugby'. He said if I signed with the ARU that I should try to come and play Super Rugby with the Waratahs. He was a lovely guy, and I had a tremendous amount of respect for his father, Steve, who's company I enjoyed so much in Origin camp the year before.

There was no big sell from Matty. He just explained his views on rugby and how he made the transition: what he found hard, what he found easy, what rugby's about and what opportunities there were on and off the field. He laid it all on the line.

The *really* important meeting came on 8 April at the mansion of ARU Chief Operations Officer Rob Clarke in the beautiful harbour-side suburb of Mosman. ARU Chief Executive Gary Flowers was also there, along with my manager, George, and his business partner, Darryl Mather.

It was a good, professional meeting. We didn't talk about money. It was just a chance for them to gauge my interest. When we left, there was a reporter from *The Daily Telegraph* waiting for us outside, along with a photographer. That pissed me off – that they knew about the meeting and where it was happening – because there were only four people who knew about it. We were about to get into George's Porsche when I turned to the photographer and asked him if he could do me a favour: 'Mate, please don't take a photo of me near a Porsche. I'm copping enough shit. I don't want to be seen near a Porsche.'

'Yeah, no worries,' the photographer laughed, turning his lens away. He was good about it.

I knew what people were saying: I was money hungry and a mercenary, putting cash ahead of everything else. Sometimes you are the face of things that aren't your fault. Because of that, I knew I was probably never going to go across. I knew I wouldn't have the instinct or the passion. I had never thought about code-jumping before that headline in 2005, which speaks volumes about my thought process at the time. I had a fair bit of curiosity from the initial conversations, but deep down I knew I wanted to stay in league.

I am not pleading complete innocence in the whole process, because after my curiosity had subsided I knew there was a certain amount of leveraging being done on my behalf. It was never conducted in an unprofessional way, but I probably could have told the ARU I wasn't coming across a couple of weeks earlier. While the ongoing talks represented bargaining power for us, it was also highlighting a bigger issue for the game, and one that still remains: the restriction of players' earnings outside the game. To the NRL's credit, though, I think they have acknowledged the inability of players to profit from external revenue sources, and I am sure it will be of mutual benefit for both parties when the new broadcast rights deal is done.

Players aren't crying, 'Poor ol me, I'm not getting enough money.' Players earn good money, but in comparison to what they *should* be getting, in comparison to what the game as a product *earns*, it should be much more. Because of that, player managers are looking for an edge in negotiations. But, again, I think the independent commission will work with the players to rectify this.

Joey knew what I was going through. His column in *The Sunday Telegraph* nailed the problem in front of me, and for others:

> Mark Gasnier has a massive decision to make. I know because I've been through it. There are so many things to weigh up when there is an offer to switch codes. If it's anything like what it was for me, he will be changing his mind from one day to the next about whether to stay or go to rugby union.
>
> He will be asking himself if he has achieved all he wants to achieve in league and whether rugby can offer him a different and enjoyable challenge that is worth making the switch for. There are the lifestyle changes and the cultural differences to consider. Then there is the money. The Australian Rugby Union seemingly has a bottomless pit.
>
> Our game doesn't enjoy that luxury and I don't care who you are or who you work for, if someone comes along willing to double your salary, you are going to seriously listen to them.
>
> There is a solution.
>
> Reward our elite players for reaching representative status by paying them accordingly. I don't know how

much the code makes out of the State of Origin series each year, but the players should be getting a far greater portion of the pie than they receive at the moment. That would automatically boost their incomes without affecting what they earn from their clubs.

At one stage, Dragons Chief Executive Peter Doust described the offer on the table as being similar to 'telephone numbers'. It's true, they were offering good money, but it wasn't telephone number money.

I do want to stress that, to the ARU's credit, when their offer arrived, the money didn't come with massive guarantees or anything like that. The figure was about $800,000 a season, but I would've had to earn it. I would've had to play every Test, every Waratahs match, to reach the dollars and cents that were being offered.

The other issue was whether I should be picked in representative sides if I was about to turn my back – as many were describing it – on the game. They were saying the same thing about Trent Barrett. It was a stupid argument – we hadn't agreed to anything. Only discussions had occurred, and everything was being played out in the media.

Then the criticism came from a little closer to home. A couple of reporters managed to track down Uncle Reg. Nathan Brown had evoked the Gasnier surname when he said that I had 'one of the most famous names ever to play the game, and that shouldn't be lost on the game'. I had been linked to Reg for so long, but by this point in my career I felt that I was starting to achieve enough to earn a name in my own right. Still, I was never surprised when the bloodline was raised.

In one interview, Uncle Reg said, 'Yeah, I'd support him if he moved to rugby. I do know what the Gasnier name means to people in rugby league, so it wouldn't be the greatest thing if he left, but it's not my place to stand in his way.' When he was asked if the ARU's offer held more weight than any great name of the game, Reg replied, 'All I know is that you're a long time retired. Mark doesn't ring me; what Mark does is his own business. I don't know what he's doing. He's doing what he wants to do, and that's fair enough.'

Then, in another interview, he was asked if I should be allowed to play for Australia in the upcoming Anzac Test against the Kiwis. 'I wouldn't pick him either, not if he's going to rugby union, and I don't know if he is or not,' he said. 'Of course I would like to see him stay, but I've played football, I've had my time, he's going through his now. If he decided to go to rugby union then he has [turned his back on the game]. And I played both codes.'

In the end, the threat of not allowing me to play rep footy subsided. The focus was turning onto the NRL and Chief Executive David Gallop. It opened a larger debate about the salary cap and how much money the game's leading players were receiving. Was it too much or not enough?

Ricky Stuart had been handed the job as coach of the Kangaroos when Wayne Bennett had stood down after we had lost the Tri Nations final to New Zealand in England the previous November. While we were bashed in that game 24–0, Wayne had been great for me on the tour. I was splitting up with my partner of six years and spending a lot of time on the phone, and Wayne is great at letting you focus on your football when you have to, then deal with the rest of your life away from it.

Having won the Origin series with NSW the year before, Ricky was the logical choice to replace him. But he had concerns that the code-switching distractions and interest from the ARU would affect my game in the Anzac Test against the Kiwis in early May. When I got into camp, Sticky pulled me aside.

'Gaz, are you sweet to play this match?' he asked.

'Of course, I am,' I said, puzzled.

'All I want to know is are you sweet to play?' he asked again.

'It's Australia. Of course I am.'

'Of course,' Stick said and then laughed.

I was puzzled, but then as he walked off he turned around and threw in a smug comment: 'Mate, you won't even get your jersey dirty over in that fucking game.'

He walked away and we started the training session. There wasn't another word spoken about it.

Luckily, I had had Stick in Origin the year before. I knew what he was like and how passionate he was about the game of rugby league – which is ironic because he had started his own career in rugby union and was a dual-international. He's a funny, honest, down-to-earth bloke, and that's why I love him.

In one game, he helped restore pride and passion in the Australian jumper after many said international football was dead. The Kangaroos beat the Kiwis 50–12 in Andrew Johns' final Test played at Suncorp Stadium in Brisbane. Two days after the Test, Trent announced that he was signing with Wigan as we had all predicted.

I could never bag the Dragons, because they had always been so good to me, but I was really upset that Baz was leaving. He was an integral part of our club and the last person I wanted to see walk away. Baz had been through a lot. The face-slapping incident with Nathan Brown didn't help. In the end, he and Browny probably didn't see eye to eye. I reckon Baz was over the club to some extent, and with three young kids he wanted to just get out.

But that doesn't mean it was easy to see him leave. He was our captain, our five-eighth, and he had had a massive influence on my career, right from the moment I came into grade. His long passing game made me look better than I was at times, but above all was a champion person.

That's why the comments from Johnny Raper about Baz not being fit enough to wear the No.6 jumper angers me so much. After making them – that very week – he had the hide to come into the dressing-room at Kogarah Oval. Trent had a blinder. Johnny came in and shook everyone's hand and said, 'Congratulations.'

That was and still is something you have to learn to cop as a Dragons player. Because of the club's rich history, there were always legendary figures that the media would regularly go to for comment. And Johnny was their go-to man. It happened every year, and we thought it was a joke: another one of the past players would come out with an adverse comment about us. I can tell you, it definitely fuelled the fire within and brought us closer together.

In particular, we wanted to rally around blokes like Trent and go out and play well for them. It was a respect thing. I know the guys were good to me when I felt I was copping it. They always said, 'Gaz, you know, you're sweet, mate. Don't worry about it.'

My teammates knew what the situation was. Many people in the game thought I was definitely gone. That I had done a deal with ARU, and all that needed to come out next was an announcement: I was gone.

But I was never gone.

On the other side of town, the ARU thought that I wasn't coming. They set a deadline, the deadline passed, and they withdrew their offer. A week later it was back on the table.

It took until the end of May to announce that I was staying with league, mainly because George had invested a lot of time and effort into finding third-party agreements to supplement the Dragons' base offer of $350,000 per season. Those agreements were for the amounts of $100,000, $125,000, $50,000 and $25,000. I signed letters of intent with those companies, and the NRL signed off on the deals. The total value of the contract was $650,000 per season over five years. A total of $3.25 million.

So I had a decision to make. George had said for a few weeks that we would get the bottom line off both offers and then make the call. It wasn't one I agonised over. When I announced that I was staying at the Dragons, I said, 'Rugby union had a lot of lures, but in saying that so did league as well. I haven't won a premiership, I've never played in a Grand Final and, as far as I see it, I'm only just starting. I'd like to have a good four or five seasons under my belt straight and see what sort of player I am then.'

Privately, the ARU said they understood, but Rob Clarke said it was a money decision. 'People should remember we did withdraw our offer to Mark,' he was quoted saying. 'We did that when the salary cap increases for next year had not been finalised and he wanted more time to make a decision. So, in the end, I can't help but feel he stayed for the money in league. We had a fair offer on the table, but we believe St George Illawarra bent over backwards, and the salary cap increases gave them the chance to keep him in the game.'

I think they were a bit peeved off about the delay in negotiations and felt like they were being leveraged against the Dragons, and I can see where they are coming from. I think ultimately I was a bit blinded by the money being negotiated, and when I actually thought about my future in depth, I kept referring back to the statement I'd made earlier: 'I'd never thought about code-jumping until I saw that headline.' That summed up to me where my heart lay.

So rugby league was the game I was going to play. The Dragons was the club I was going to play for. For life.

The following night we played the Knights in Newcastle. It turned out to be a great night for me, scoring the first try and then setting up another as we went on to win 38–12.

Browny said afterwards that the contract negotiations had been a distraction. 'The last two games Gaz has played for us, he's dropped the ball in the same situation he scored in tonight,' he said. 'He's dropped five in the past three weeks. I have no doubt all that doesn't help, you know? It's a big decision. Gaz tonight was the best game he's played for us in at least four weeks, four or five games.'

I didn't agree with that at all. Throughout the season, Browny had asked if the interest from the ARU had been an unwanted distraction, and I had said it had not. 'I've tried to play well throughout the whole year,' I said. 'Through the week I'd sit down and think about things and talk to people. But come two days before the game, I stopped everything and focused solely on what was ahead.'

I thought I *was* playing well. In fact, I thought I was playing as well as I ever had. And I was enjoying the game again, *without* injury. Away from footy, my head was in a good place too. Oh well, sometimes coaches over-analyse things. Sorry, Browny!

I must have been doing something right because Phil Gould had called me the best centre he'd seen, which was a massive rap coming from a person of his calibre and who'd spent so much time in the game. I was really humbled.

Gus was also responsible for providing my teammates with plenty of ammunition when he described my step as a 'shimmy'. The 'shimmy-shimmy-*whoosh!*' to be precise. My long-term boot sponsor Adidas – who were great to me throughout my whole career from the age of 17 – gave me a pair of boots with those very words embossed on the side.

I gave them up straightaway, but it didn't stop the boys at training from giving me a hammering about them.

Midway through the year, the only downside had been the way we had lost the Origin series. Up until that season, NSW had won three series in a row. Our dominance over Queensland was considered detrimental to the concept. We won the first game in Sydney, through a miraculous field goal at the end of the game from Brett Finch, the funny little Roosters half-back who had been the seventh choice because of injury and suspension, and who only joined us the night before kick-off.

We lost game two in Brisbane and, as we headed to Melbourne for the decider, my move to five-eighth came quicker than I thought. After the loss in game two, NSW selectors decided to drop Braith Anasta and bring me into the role.

I'd played a few games at five-eighth around this time because Baz had been suspended. It was a dress rehearsal for next year, and Browny had actually told them not to pick me in Origin. He knew it was going to take time for me to get used to that role.

I have to admit, the whole idea of moving into the No.6 jumper permanently wasn't something I was completely comfortable with. A selfish part of me knew that I had established myself as a capable centre, but at the same time it was a new challenge and Browny threw it out there, thinking it was best for the team. It's not like I told him at any stage that I was a bit iffy about it all. I said, 'Okay, I'll do it. If that's what you think is best for the team, I'll do it.'

The heartening thing was to learn that some great players,

like Laurie Daley, thought I was NSW's long-term five-eighth. I wasn't sure, but it was a nice endorsement. For the decider, though, I knew I was going to be more of a second full-back than a traditional five-eighth, as I had played the position in the previous weeks with the Dragons. Half-back Craig Gower pretty much ran everything, which allowed me to float around the field and look for opportunities.

History shows that we lost that game when full-back Brett Hodgson threw a loose pass with six minutes to go, and Queensland captain Darren Lockyer scooped it up and scored. Now that I've finished my career, I can honestly say that, apart from the loss to the Wests Tigers in the 2005 preliminary final, this was the most upset I had been after a game.

The disappointing way we finished off the season was right up there as well. We had been sitting in second position, behind leaders Melbourne Storm, in early July. A calf injury meant I was in one week and on the sidelines the next. But by the time the home-and-away season was over, we finished in sixth position and needed to win every week to stay alive in the semifinals. It was now or never.

We shocked Brisbane at Suncorp Stadium in the first week of the finals, winning 20–4, but I'd copped a knee in the hip from Broncos player Casey Maguire, and it placed me in severe doubt all week for the semifinal against Manly at the Sydney Football Stadium. I didn't play, but the boys did well to beat them 28–0.

Here we were again: one game away from the Grand Final, this time against the Melbourne Storm, the minor premiers who had become a strong team under the guidance of coach Craig Bellamy, as well as under the emergence of a young centre named Greg Inglis.

We were confident, though. Half-back Matty Head was in really good form. So was Trent, who knew every game could be his last for us. Everyone was playing well. I was desperate to play, but the hip injury was bad. I had about four or five needles in order to play, but ultimately we came up short against a very good outfit that executed a lot better than we did on the night. Melbourne won 24–10.

How devastated were we after that loss? Very. Personally, I felt like we'd let Trent down a fair bit. When people give so much to the club, you think they deserve a fairytale ending. In rugby league, they rarely happen.

TEN

UNCLE REG

Uncle Reg came to see me play a junior grand final at Kogarah Oval during the early 1990s. After the match, he came up to me and passed on a few words. 'I'm not going to tell you what to do,' he said. 'My only advice is to just enjoy it. Make the most of it.' That's about the only advice he's given me – and the only advice I've needed from him.

There is a misconception out there that Reg and I have never got on. Nothing could be further from the truth. Reg and I have never fallen out. Sure, there are no rosy stories about how close we've been. As I said before, Uncle Reg was the bloke I saw at Christmas and other family functions. We weren't very close, like many uncles and nephews, but there's definitely no animosity. When I hear that misconception, I find it weird. Gossip columns haven't helped over the years, hinting at a rift that isn't there. The simple fact is I have seen

Reg plenty of times over the last few years. I see Aunty Maureen, and I see my cousins Peter and Kelly too. They still live in the Sutherland Shire.

When he gave me that simple advice that day, I could see where he was coming from by handing me such a general statement. If I was offering a kid advice these days, which I have done in the past at a function or a school ceremony, I wouldn't want to fill their heads with technical jargon. Players are who they are. They have their own instincts, their own plan about how they want to approach their football and their careers. Unless they ask you a specific question about a specific area of the game, you have to be general and broad in your advice.

At no stage throughout my career did I feel a need to seek out Reg and ask for guidance. In modern-day rugby league, I had enough coaches – four or five at some stages. There were enough voices in my ear without having to find another one. There comes a point when you have to simplify things. You can have technical game plans, but you have to know your role and simplify it so you can execute it correctly. You can't go into a game with a hundred things in your head. One thing that makes footballers good footballers is their adaptability.

I didn't speak to Reg much over my career, but that wasn't because I didn't feel comfortable seeking his advice. Look at the gap between when he played and when I played – there is 30 years between us. I loved speaking to Reg about what it was like in his day. It's funny to hear about his preparation compared to what mine had been during my career. Reg would have steak and eggs in the morning and polish his boots. I'd have ice baths and stretching sessions. The eras had changed too much for us to relate to each other on the technical side of rugby league. But there are certain principles that span the eras, like effort and commitment.

I don't mean any disrespect to the surname when I say this, but I am me. Reg is Reg. It would piss me off that some people would say what the Gasnier name meant. Sometimes, it did give me the shits. I never showed it and I never spoke to anyone about it, but it did piss me off that people would presume who I was playing for. I would like to think I was always diplomatic about it during my career, but I can talk about it now.

And this is it: I know that I represent Reg's legacy. I know that it's part of the tradition of the game and the club and their golden era. I know and appreciate and respect all of that. It is actually an honour from a football perspective. But I have always believed I represent something more than that. When I have represented the Gasnier name, I have been representing John and Janene Gasnier. And my brothers – Gavin, Brent and Dean. It's something that I've always felt passionately about. Family is everything to me. That's why I felt so bad in 2004 with the phone-call scandal during the Origin camp. I had represented my immediate family in the worst kind of way.

Of course I know Uncle Reg was an unbelievable player, arguably the best ever. Of course he was the one who put our surname in the spotlight. That has never been in dispute. What he did must've been so incredible given all the accolades he gets. It wasn't until Dad showed me the tapes of when he played, and the farther I progressed in the game, that I fully realised his standing.

He played for St George from 1959 to 1967, and was a major part of their run of 11 premierships in a row. He played with the likes of Johnny Raper, Norm Provan and Graeme Langlands, and all those wonderful players who are a part of Dragons folklore. He played a record 36 Test matches, captained his country eight times, and when *Rugby League Week* named their first four Immortals during the early 1980s, he was one of them.

Was I angered at the constant comparisons? At having my career considered in light of what Reg did? At regularly being referred to as 'the nephew of Immortal Reg Gasnier'? Definitely not. Sometimes it wore on me, but then I had to think about why they're doing it. This guy had done so much in the game – he's an Immortal. Of course they are going to refer to the link between generations. I played in the same position, for the same club. Those were things I accepted. But I always knew in the back of my mind that I wanted to create my own name. And like everything in life, you have to earn it.

I also understand what might have fuelled the speculation about a fall out between Reg and me: his quote saying that I shouldn't be picked in the Kangaroos team if I was going to sign with the ARU.

Obviously, this is a private family matter and I won't go into detail, but Reg's wife, Maureen, and his children, Peter and Kelly, called me when those comments came out. Reg wasn't well at the time. He had recently had a fall and had only just returned from a stint in hospital. A journo had contacted him at the family home.

The family rang Mum to say that his comments had been taken out of context. While I had learnt to block out a lot of what was written and broadcast, I was definitely aware of the story. By then, though, I'd learnt how everything in the media works. I understood how they were the kings of beating stuff up.

They got a comment; they made a story out of it. For me, I could sit back and see the big picture. After this story started to take off, I just sat back and put everything into context. It is truly amazing how little things can be made into big stories. It's smart what they do: they create public debate that ultimately leads to sales and more revenue.

I had it pretty clear in my own mind, by the time all this was going on, that I was going to stay in league. It was just a matter of playing football and getting on with things. In hindsight, I wonder what he would've thought if the Gasnier name ended up playing rugby union in a pink jersey in France?

ELEVEN

PECS, HAMMYS, QUADS, CALVES...

At the end of 2006 and early 2007 I thought my luck was heading in the right direction. I met a beautiful girl by the name of Claudine, got named co-captain along with Benny Hornby and Jason Ryles, and my body was feeling fresher than ever. That's when the curse of injury struck me down again – and this time it would be the worst of my career.

It was the Charity Shield match against South Sydney, with an injury that barely hurt.

There had been plenty of talk about my move to five-eighth during the off-season. I knew it was going to take time. So did coach Nathan Brown. I'd been a part of the Kangaroos' Tri Nations victory, having beaten New Zealand in the final in golden-point extra time, and he'd given me a good break. I had a really good pre-season – one of my better ones – and was feeling really excited, probably the best I had felt in my career. Mentally, I was in a great place.

Apart from the handful of matches in 2006 with Trent Barrett out injured, and game three of the Origin series, I had worn the No.6 jumper on my back just once – playing in the Harold Matthews Cup for the Dragons many, many years ago. Laurie Daley, one of the great five-eighths, came out publicly and said I could become as dominant as Broncos captain Darren Lockyer in the position. I didn't know about that, but I thought the experiment was working well in training.

Ben Hornby had moved from full-back to half-back because of injury concerns about Mat Head. Wes Naiqama and Matty Cooper were playing in the centres with Josh Morris at full-back. 'The switch with Gaz going to five-eighth is going to give us more chances,' Coops said before the Charity Shield. 'It'll give us a chance to get a good combination between the two of us. He's a great player, and if I can run off Gaz and score a few tries off him, it's going to be good. I don't think a win is really important. The thing that's really important is we go out there and do things we've been practising at training.'

Having missed the first trial match of the season against the Bulldogs, Browny wanted me to play the entire game to start the process of learning the position.

Then the weirdest thing happened. In the 60th minute, team physio and good mate Andrew Gray came up to me on the field. 'Gaz!' he shouted. 'Five more minutes and then you're off!'

No worries, I thought. I actually didn't want to go off.

Three minutes later, Souths centre Nigel Vagana took the ball up off a scrum. I'd gone around his legs, one of my team-mates had gone high, and Nigel had gone through. At the point of contact my arm bent back and I felt pins and needles down it. Nothing major – those types of things happen all the time in the course of a game during a season. I wasn't in any serious pain and didn't think much of it.

About six minutes later, Souths scored a try. We were behind the goal posts and I said to Drew, 'I've got pins and needles but it doesn't feel like a burner. It feels weak.' He did a couple of things, and then I felt him put his fingers up underneath my pectoral muscle.

'You're off!' he ordered.

'Nah, mate,' I said. 'It's cool, just give me a bit longer. There are still some things I want to practise.'

'No way,' he said.

Before I knew it, I was sitting in the dressing-room and the team doctor was running some tests. Drew's face on the field had said it all: it was a serious injury.

'Do a one-arm push-up on the wall,' the doctor said.

So I tried . . . and headbutted the wall. It turns out I'd ruptured my pectoral muscle, but nobody was keen to tell me how serious the injury was. The question was the extent of the tear. Scans the next day revealed I'd torn the muscle, the ligament and the tendon – all off the bone.

Browny described the injury as a 'tragedy' when he broke the news in the media conference.

'I'm shattered,' was all I could manage. 'I can't believe it.'

★

Injuries. I had so many of them during the course of my 12 seasons of professional football that I couldn't tell you how many or exactly what I've done, but here's a snapshot:

Broken leg. Dislocated fingers. Snapped foot ligaments. Hammy and quadricep tears. Ankle operations. Calves – so many calves. Broken collarbone. Wrist reconstruction. Knee cap taken out. Ruptured pectoral muscle. I even fractured my back three times when I was younger! Must be those chalky bones. Who knows?

I once tore my arse. Can you believe that? My physio said I'm the only person he's ever known in his life who has done it. I went to take off during a sprint in a training game and felt something twinge. I'd torn one of the small muscles inside the pelvis. It's best described as a 'deep pelvic muscle tear' and you only usually find it among tennis players, who are stepping and stretching laterally and at angles the human body shouldn't be pushed to. In my case, it was the force I was generating from stepping off one foot to cut sideways. The radiologist laughed when he saw my torn arse: 'Well, I haven't seen that one before.' I missed one week.

I'd missed several weeks, over several seasons, in my career, but nothing was as confronting or hard to swallow as the ruptured pectoral muscle. The early assumption was that I would be out for the season, but then it was downgraded to 19 weeks on the sideline. That would get me back a month out from the play-offs. I made it clear in my head: *I want to be back for the finals.*

Two former Dragons players – Luke Bailey and Scott Geddes – had suffered the same injury. Our doctor, Paul

Arnett, told me it would be a five- to six-month rehabilitation, but Bails came back from a very similar injury in 2004 in 20 weeks.

I spoke to him the night after the Charity Shield. He said he'd ignored the medical advice to wait as long as possible, and even signed a waiver agreeing not to sue his surgeon before returning to the field. I was in a similar frame of mind, I was that desperate to get back.

The heartening thing from such a terrible situation was how many people contacted me to give me their best wishes – from teammates past and present to players from other teams, including Andrew Johns, who had plenty of his own injury dramas in the past. But there was no escaping how dreadful I felt. As I said to *The Daily Telegraph*: 'I am so devastated. I put so much into the off-season. I have done much more work than ever before, with the co-captaincy and the positional change to five-eighth. I just can't believe this has happened to me.'

People have often asked me, 'What is it like to grapple with all those injuries? What does it do to your mental state?'

Well, it messes with you. I'm generally a positive person and always up-beat. But it's hard to hide the frustration when you have setbacks with your body. As I've said, you need consistent games under your belt to play your best football, and when you're injured it's hard not to feel like you're letting your teammates down.

The worst thing for me when injury ravaged a whole season was that I could see myself progressing every time I had a decent pre-season with the team. Mentally, that really challenges you, constantly trying to stay positive. You get frustrated and depressed. Then you realise there's no use getting frustrated, because that isn't going to solve anything. You've got to let things heal first, and then you've got to do the hard work to get back. There is no other alternative.

Every player with long-term injuries knows what it's like to not be a part of the main squad. The squad where you belong. While you still feel part of the team, it's not the same as being a contributing member week in and week out. And that gets to you. The other challenge is that you have to constantly prove yourself when you come back, and that's very draining as well. Some people are blessed with a smooth run over their career. I definitely wasn't.

I know of other players, especially late in their careers, who were concerned that they would never come back as the same player. I was never one of them. I'd done a lot of training and I was always keen to get back on the field, and with that desire and commitment came confidence. I didn't question myself too much, even if others did.

Not only did a handful of players text me their support. One of the first people to contact me was Claudine, who I had been on several dates with up until then, and she wanted to see if I was okay. I do believe that things happen for a reason, and if you are a good person they are generally for the better. I think 2007 reinforced that for me. My injury meant that I had a lot more time, and it allowed Claude and I to grow a lot closer. It also gave me a lot of experience in television with Channel 9, which has helped me greatly to this day.

I should clear this up now: Claudine is from a French family, but she did not grow up in France. I did not meet her there, as some people seem to wrongly assume because our relationship only really came into the public spotlight when I was headed overseas to play rugby.

Her mum, Irene, and father, Jean-Pierre, were born in France – Irene in Paris and her dad in a little town called Gabarret in the south-west of the country. Her family moved to Australia when her elder sister was five, and Claude was born in Dural, NSW, before the family moved to Newport on Sydney's northern beaches. For years, they owned a French restaurant called Bonnachere across the road from the iconic Newport Arms Hotel.

By mid-2007, Claude and I were pretty much joined at the hip, which would have made the service stations happy as Claude lived in Newport and I lived in Cronulla.

It was early July when I walked onto the training field for the first time. It had been a long road back. I'd been on a restricted weights program: I could only do moderate weight bench press on the floor. All shoulder rehab was restricted in weight as well, so while I was getting strong I still had a bit to go.

I was doing a lot of running, so fitness wasn't a problem. Andrew Gray and Marcus Kain worked tirelessly to help me get back when I did, creating programs, adapting to my progress and allowing for adequate recovery. I would sometimes get physio treatments at 7 in the evening at Andrew's house – that's the level of commitment these guys had to getting me back.

'It puts a bit of excitement back into training,' I told *The Sun-Herald*. 'Now that I can see a bit of light at the end of the tunnel, I'm starting to get excited. I'm putting my mind to getting back as quickly and as safely as I can. I'm not getting too far ahead of myself, because in a perfect world I'll be back in five weeks, but things don't always work out like that. I'm going to continue with my rehab and, if it continues to progress the way it is, I'll start to get excited. If you ask me in four weeks and I haven't had a setback and I'm lifting heavy weights, I'll be really excited.'

Then they asked me what position I wanted to play. Did I want to return to the five-eighth role, which had lasted all of 63 minutes this season in the Charity Shield? 'I'm just happy to get a football in my hand,' I said.

The truth was it didn't matter what I wanted. Other players had been battling their own injury problems. We had been without injured Ben Hornby, Wes Naiqama, Mathew Head, Simon Woolford, Dean Young, Ashton Sims and Brett Morris for most of the season. And it was reflected on the competition ladder. I was pencilled in for a return in Round 19 against Penrith – seven weeks ahead of schedule – and at that point of the season we were third-last on the ladder. I was playing next to a young half named Jamie Soward, who had been unwanted at the Roosters but who would go on to become a very important player for the Dragons.

We ended up beating the Panthers 38–20 that night. After the game, I tried to give some insight into the relief I felt to be just out there again, and how tough it had been not playing. 'It's like a big part of your life gets taken away, you get a bit lost. Now I can go back and surf tomorrow morning guilt-free, and my shoulder feels good. I'm just excited about playing footy. Unfortunately, it's happened to me for a fair few years where I've missed a lot of football – I don't take it for granted anymore. I think the last two years I've enjoyed my football a lot more than I did when I was younger. I probably took it for granted a bit when I was younger, but I really appreciate it now.' And because I had taken on a lot more responsibility with the co-captaincy, I felt a real sense of ownership.

Despite the win against the Panthers, our form remained very patchy. We continued to have a heap of injuries, which made for a bit of a makeshift team, and a lot of people were leaving next year. After the Penrith game, we were set to take on the Bulldogs. It was before that match that I suffered the deep pelvis injury. 'I took off to sprint and got a big pain in the bum – literally,' I said, much to the amusement of the journos who were there. I was actually shattered – I had just returned from my torn pec. Nineteen weeks on the sideline and now I had *this* problem. An injury the radiologist hadn't even *seen*.

After we lost the Round 23 match against the Cowboys in Townsville, Browny approached me in the rooms. 'Is everything all right?' he asked. Then I laid it out to him how frustrated I was on the field. I moved back to the centres for the rest of the season.

We didn't make the finals.

★

But it wasn't all bad.

For starters, I made the Prime Minister's XIII to face Papua New Guinea in Port Moresby, played just a week before the Grand Final between Melbourne and Manly. The push to be selected for that team had come from Ricky Stuart, the Kangaroos' coach. There were also spots up for grabs for a Test match against New Zealand in Wellington the next month.

Ricky put a lot of faith in me, and I owe him heaps of credit for my representative career. He taught me responsibility and how to take ownership over my life and football when I was only 26. When Roosters backrower Craig Fitzgibbon had to pull out of the side because of an ankle injury, I was installed as Test captain. As a kid, you dream about playing for your country, let alone leading them out, so I was very proud.

The game was chaos. We had led 20–0 at half-time, but the Kumuls ended up coming back and the match finished in a 24–all draw. Referee Gavin Bagder was worried about getting out of the airport alive, so few calls went the home side's way. Not that we cared. We were actually over there for a greater cause: spreading the safe-sex message and the importance of wearing condoms. Papua New Guinea's HIV-positive population is second to Africa, and rugby league is the country's number one sport. The locals listened to us and, along with Johnny Howard's donation of nearly $138 million, we were trying to get the point across. However, one of the biggest problems is that a high percentage of infection comes from rape. It's a desperate situation.

With the great Darren Lockyer out injured, there was some talk of me filling out his vacant Australian No.6 jumper, but in the end they gave it to Greg Bird, who was playing for Cronulla at the time. I was selected in the centres, back where I belonged.

Playing for my country against the Kiwis would be a great way to underline a forgettable year. Then, in the 24th minute of the Test, my opposite centre Steve Matai tried to put a shot on me – as he does – and it went horribly wrong. He hit me high and knocked me out – cold. I had to be taken from the field in a medicab, and I took no further part in the game. The concussion was so bad that I didn't regain consciousness until the second half. Even then, the trainers had to convince me that we weren't playing the game in Melbourne.

Referee Steve Ganson sent Matai from the field. Playing against 12 men, with a backline that featured the likes of Johnathan Thurston, Billy Slater and Greg Inglis, we racked up a 58–0 scoreline, smashing all records for the trans-Tasman clash.

Of course, I don't remember much of it. Ricky was absolutely filthy: 'It was late and it was a cheap shot,' Stick said. 'Late and cheap like that is not good for the game. I don't mind if there's a high shot when it's a reaction. That was late. He knew where he was going.' Then a journo asked him how I was feeling. 'He thought he was in Melbourne. He's been very sick.'

I said to Stick later that I was filthy about missing out on that victory because it was raining tries and everyone got a piece of the action except me. I saw the replay of the incident, and of course he was trying to put a shot on, but that's just the way he plays. I don't think it was intentional. That's football sometimes.

It's true to say that I had been targeted a bit throughout my career. After my strong seasons in 2005 and 2006, every team clamped down on me. Every defensive structure I played against, the centre would get wide outside of me, no matter how wide I ran, and he'd just wait for the third man from the inside to cover his inside shoulder, generally the five-eighth or half-back.

I have to admit, it was pretty annoying. You'd try to beat him on the outside, but you would have only two metres of space to work in. The winger is right on the line. In saying that, footy was changing. You really had to be on the front foot, getting a roll on before the defence was set. Before, you would have set plays, but now you need to recognise the quick play ball. Then it's up to the dummy half, or the halves, to realise whether the opportunity is out wide.

Not everything went wrong that year. At the end of it, Claude and I moved into a place together in Curl Curl on Sydney's northern beaches. Things were only going from strength to strength in that regard.

TWELVE

LEAVING HOME

THE 2008 SEASON STARTED well with Browny asking me if I thought I was ready to lead the team as sole captain. I told him I thought I was ready. I'd been through so much as a player and a man at this club, and now I was ready to lead it. When he gave me the job, it was one of the proudest moments of my career. I was really humbled by it, when you consider the past players who had held it, and how far I'd come to lead the team.

'The captaincy is something that demands more out of you,' I told *The Daily Telegraph*. 'At the end of the day, I'm trying to preach certain things to the players, so I've got to lead the way. I've got to set the standard.'

I had damaged that honour in some ways because I was out after curfew early in the season. The club fined me $5000, which was not disclosed to the public at the time. The fine was fair enough. As captain, I knew I'd stuffed up in a big way. 'I sincerely apologise for the poor example I have set in this instance,' I said in a statement. 'It comes down to choices, and I have no one to blame other than myself.'

Dousty saw it as a case of being in the wrong place at the wrong time. We had also set some standards and rules as a leadership group. I had been fined purely for breaking those rules.

Are rugby league players role models? Some players say they shouldn't be, and I can understand that view to a certain extent. You're a kid, a teen, a young man growing up in society like everyone else. We shouldn't have to behave any differently, just abide by the same rules as the rest of society. But footballers are often set a different set of rules – by their coach or the club's management. Although most good coaches put the onus on the individual to act responsibly rather than place boundaries on them.

Players can whinge about it but they're the sacrifices you have to make. If the media and public weren't so interested, players wouldn't be getting paid what they do. But, of course, there's a line. I've heard players talk about the so-called 'fishbowl' existence they have to lead. Some players think they are unfairly watched and scrutinised compared to other corners of society. But I also think the so-called Generation Y players who are coming through at the moment expose themselves more than the media do, through social networking.

After living in Europe for a while and seeing what their footballers go through, rugby league in Australia doesn't come close to being a fishbowl. I really enjoyed interacting with the public when I played. The worst comments I ever got from fans were things like, 'Go the Doggies!' or 'You're going to get smashed today!' Almost all of the stuff was in good humour. When I made the decision to go to France, I had people asking why I went. Then I had to explain it to them. They can only respect that, because you are prepared to give them your time.

Australians are so approachable. They're good people. Most of the public doesn't want to take advantage of that. People feel like they can approach a high-profile player, and most of the players don't mind it either. They *shouldn't* mind it. Over my whole career, I've had so many beers with fans who I've just met out and about on the town. I enjoyed talking to them. Some people had great views and ideas about issues in the game.

Is there greater pressure on us now? When the phone call incident occurred, I realised how much interest the public takes in the game and its players. Social media brought greater *scrutiny* to all of us. Camera phones, Myspace, Facebook, Twitter – the spotlight has never shone brighter, and it is only going to get more intrusive. But people have to remember that you can manage that. Personally, I think fame is like doing a deal with the devil: it seems great at the time, but it will often come back to bite you on the bum.

But that's not pressure. The *real* pressure, if you are serious about the game, comes from you. The player. During my own career, the person who put the most pressure on me was me. Deep down, every player is the same. You don't want to let your teammates down – that is the driving force.

While being handed the captaincy was a great honour, trouble was looming. The four external third-party agreements I had signed in 2006 – worth $650,000 over five years – were owing per season, I had a base payment of $300,000 from the Dragons plus a marquee player agreement from the Dragons for $50,000, all of which were fully paid. The Dragons had honoured their contractual commitments to the dollar and on time. But the other external deals that had been struck to keep me in the game in 2006 were not. They were individually worth $100,000, $125,000, $50,000 and $25,000. As much as I'd like to, I can't reveal all the details and the names of the companies and organisations who made these commitments to me. At the time of writing I am still trying to get my money from some of them, and there are still people involved in the game. Believe me, if I could name them I would!

The most frustrating thing is that I had satisfied my end of the bargain and met every one of the commitments required as part of those arrangements. I had done my pec muscle in 2007 and still fronted everything asked of me. But nothing – half my year's wage! – had been paid.

It got to the point where enough was enough. I phoned my manager, George Mimis. 'It's been a year,' I said to him. 'What is the problem?'

It seems the deals were not as black and white as I expected them to be – they were 'letters of intent'. One of the third parties said to George that it had made the agreement with the 'best intentions' and nothing more. Because of the salary cap rules, neither the Dragons nor the NRL could guarantee the deals.

Well, it wasn't 'best intentions' as far as I was concerned. I was told it was guaranteed money that would be paid by certain dates. Some monthly, some half-yearly. I never saw a cent of it.

I felt the matter was simple: you do a deal, you do a deal. In business, that doesn't seem to be the case. After all, I had mortgages like everyone else. You budget what you buy based on your earning power. I said, 'George, I can't keep going. I'm not crying poor but something has to give. I'll have to sell something. I need to know where I'm heading.'

I could understand if things had happened, if these businesses had cashflow problems and were not been able to pay. But as far as I was aware they had the money. I had to set a deadline. There was a clause in my contract that allowed me to explore other options up until 30 June if payments had not been met. So I said to George, 'If they don't pay up by June 2008, then I have to have a back-up plan as this is the second year this has happened.'

None of this had been revealed publicly, and the way it eventually all played out in the media – and not for the first time in my career – angered me. I had to just cop it on the chin. I want to make it very clear that I would never in a million years have thought of executing the clause to negotiate elsewhere if I had been paid what was agreed to. It wasn't about getting *more* money. It was about getting money that was rightfully mine. And that is a key difference.

Initially, it looked like I was doing nothing more than looking for more money, trying to use rugby union and overseas rugby league clubs as a way to increase my earning power. That wasn't it at all. I was out of pocket, to the tune of half my pay.

The first of these stories appeared in *The Sunday Telegraph* on 11 May, revealing the get-out clause in my contract that allowed me to negotiate with overseas clubs.

We happened to be playing Parramatta at Stadium Australia in Homebush that afternoon. I was backing up from the Centenary Test at the SCG, in which I had scored an incredible try for the Kangaroos against the Kiwis because of a freaky play from Greg Inglis, who had caught the ball from a Johnathan Thurston cross-field kick and flicked it back over his head before going over the dead-ball line.

We lost the match against Parramatta in a 19–18 nailbiter, and afterwards I fronted up when the reporters approached me. I could not go into details about what was happening, because it was still very sensitive, but I did not want the same circus surrounding the interest from rugby union two years earlier – when I had signed the deals that had now made my career so murky.

'I don't want it to be déjà vu,' I told them. 'I don't think it's fair on the club or anyone. I have to explore options over there. But it's not me going out there looking for it. I've been confronted with a situation that I've had to react to, so I've done that in my best interests. Something's happened [but] I've got to be vague. I'm not going to say the exact situation and make a whole circus of this thing. I want fans to know there's no ill will. I wouldn't have backed up today [after Friday's Test] if there was. I love the club and I'm fortunate enough to be captain. It's just unfortunate a couple of things have happened.'

Peter Doust, who had been great while all this was playing out, said, 'I'm always sympathetic. Gaz and I have always got on well together and always understand each other. I'm happy to work through it with him. We want him to be here and we want him to be a Dragons man – as he does too.'

Some people were saying, 'Mate, cop it on the chin.' But the reality is I had loans to pay, investments. I would like to think I was good with my money. When you start missing loan repayments – large repayments – you get yourself into massive dramas. If I had let the situation go any further, I would've started defaulting on them.

The whole situation reopened up a debate about the salary cap and what players should be entitled to; whether they should be able to earn extra money outside of their clubs, like through sponsorships, and whether that activity should be restricted or not. We have all heard rumours about players being paid under the table, but I had never hidden anything from the NRL. The deals were all signed off by the NRL, who were across every aspect of the deal and the issues of parties not paying their commitments. It would've been easier to have worked outside of the salary cap, done the dodgy thing, but we conducted our business with all transparently – and look what it cost me.

The captaincy I had been given all on my own at the start of the season had also weighed heavily on me. If I had my time again, I would've been more open to Browny about it. I would've told him that if I take this, I might have to leave. Maybe keep the co-captains, Ben Hornby and Rylesy. I should've done it, but I couldn't talk in too much detail because of the privacy of it all. I also didn't want to let anyone down and, most of all, I was praying it didn't happen.

I'm definitely not an emotional person around others. I keep things bottled up – I'll talk to my wife and family, and that's about it – but I can say now how unbelievably honoured I was to receive the captaincy. And there was this underlying hope about taking the Dragons into the future and one day holding that trophy above my head.

Deep down, though, I knew what was brewing. And it scared me. 'I'm worried about it,' I said to Claude. 'What if I have to walk away from all of this?' I was captain of the club that I loved, the club that I had played for since I was a kid. I was numb.

With the clause to negotiate with other clubs now enacted, I started to look elsewhere. I had spoken to Craig Gower, who I knew from representative camps and had gone the year before to French club Bayonne. There was also interest from other French rugby clubs, including Biarritz. George engaged French agent Laurent Quaglia to speak to the French clubs, while there was also interest from Super League side Catalans. There was talk about signing with the ARU, which wasn't true. After all that had happened, I wanted to get out of here. I'd prayed and hoped the uncertainty around my contract would fix itself, but when I knew that it wasn't going to, I didn't want to hang around Australia.

All this anxiety directly translated to how I performed on the field. Sometimes I'd play well, but deep down I knew I couldn't play consistent footy. I was in a bad place. All the different scenarios were unfolding before me.

Meanwhile, I still wasn't getting paid and being bagged as money hungry in the process. I was shattered and struggling, and the only person who saw it more clearly than anyone was Claude. I had shingles. I was losing weight. I didn't want to admit to any of this because I'm a proud person.

It came to a head before the second game of the Origin series. It was a really bad week; I thought I had handled it well, but in hindsight I didn't. Two days before the match, I had told Ewen McKenzie that I would be joining him at Stade Francais in Paris.

My form that night mirrored exactly what was going on in my life, with Greg Inglis running around me like I wasn't even there. I was frustrated and, despite not wanting to shift the blame, events off the field were proving too much.

It was only when I arrived back in Sydney, when we signed the contracts and faxed them to Stade Francais, that the deal was officially done. That's when I made the phone call to Peter Doust. He was really good about it and supportive. He was trying to help me in every way he could. That was the silly thing: the club and I were fine. We were working in the one direction. Players usually leave when there's a breakdown between them and the club. That wasn't the case this time. Peter Doust and the Dragons helped just as much as my manager to get things resolved.

'At least now you've made a decision; you can move on,' Claude said. 'It's out there now.' It was a relief to have my future known and sorted, but it wasn't the decision I had wanted. The best outcome would've been to be paid and continue playing for the Dragons. Even half of it.

The last chapter was played out at a press conference at the St George Leagues Club. I had purposely put it off until after the third Origin match, because I didn't want to detract from the publicity surrounding the series.

When I made the announcement, I commented that 'I'm not going to be missed that much'. I honestly believed that. I'll cop the blame and absorb – no dramas – but I know what the truth is. Yes, it wasn't nice to hear that the split was my fault, but I knew the real situation and had to make a stand. It had reached the point where I couldn't stay. If I had stayed and the money still hadn't been paid a year later, everyone would have said, 'Well, fuck off to France.' My credibility had taken a pounding, and staying would've made it worse.

The thing that pissed me off the most was the perception, driven by stories in the media, that I was going to France to apparently escape the 'fishbowl' existence. It was utter bullshit and made me look like a sook. That type of thinking is flawed.

It wasn't the fishbowl – it was the money. Nothing more. I wasn't getting paid, and there was a principle at stake. I had set dates in place and when they hadn't come to the party by those deadlines, I knew they were never going to come to the party. I would rather not have been promised those deals in 2006 – at least I would have known where I stood. The decision would've been made there and then.

People often ask me who was to blame for my getting into this predicament. It's a good question, because for a long time I didn't know *who* I was angry at. Maybe all of us involved were to blame. In reality I think the functioning of the rules of the NRL in many respects created the headache I had to endure. Either way, it's a huge lesson to everyone involved, unfortunately at my expense. But I don't think you can specifically blame one person. I don't know the details of those negotiations. What I do know is that after I made the decision to leave the game at the end of the 2008 season, I had to try to let it go and not remain bitter about it – not that everyone could do the same.

Some were bitter that I left. Some Dragons fans were angry that Josh Morris was leaving the club to play with the Bulldogs because of salary cap pressure. If I had left earlier, they could've kept him. But how was I going to stop that? Do you think I wanted this to happen? Do you think I wanted to leave? That's why I can't see the value in some people's comments. I never spoke about a lot of things when I left – I felt like I didn't have any credibility and the timing wasn't right.

Some thought I should never come back. Gorden Tallis, the former Dragons, Broncos, Queensland and Australian forward, ripped into me: 'Mark Gasnier is a wonderful player, but if he is so driven by money that he wants to go and play rugby union in France, I say au revoir. I like the guy, but in the end rugby league has done more than enough to keep him in the NRL. If he still wants to go, hand his Test, Origin and Dragons jumpers to a kid that wants to be here. In the end the NRL and the Dragons have bent over backwards to keep him in Australia. They have given him a five-year deal and made him close to the highest paid player in the game. The simple fact is rugby league can't afford to give Gasnier any more. And if the sport makes an exception for him, then what happens next time a Greg Inglis or an Israel Folau comes off contract and starts making the same threats?'

I remember the comments as clear as day. Gorden is managed by George as well, so he should've known a bit more of the facts. I'm not trying to sound like a wise old man, but I used to sit back and feel comfortable in the fact that I knew the truth. Now, if I ever get asked an opinion about something, I am careful in my reply because this whole circus made me realise that nothing is black and white, nothing is simple. It is wrong to pass judgement when you don't know all the facts. When people were ripping into me, I knew that they would know the truth some day.

Ricky Stuart was also very angry with me. I had spoken to him before the Centenary Test about what was happening, but not in great detail. He'd said to think about my career and where I was going, but those decisions had really been taken out of my hands.

When I made the decision to leave, I tried to ring Ricky but he brushed my call. I understood that. I left a message. We'd been through so much together, for NSW and then Australia, so I knew time would heal those wounds. That was Sticky being Sticky. I've always respected him. It was a sensitive time, too. Sonny Bill Williams had walked out on the Bulldogs at the end of July, and it was seen as another money-hungry player wanting his payday. I'm not going to judge Sonny Bill, because I don't know all the circumstances.

I was also dealing with a considerable amount of anger at this time. I genuinely believed, once I had made the decision to leave, my rugby league career was over. I was never coming back. I hoped that in some strange way I would play another game at Kogarah. But, as angry as I was, it was a sentimental hope.

Am I still bitter? A part of me thinks we could've won a premiership in 2009. Another makes me think about how many more Tests and Origins I could've played. I look back now, at how things played out, and I could've held the honour of captaining the Dragons until the day I retired.

But I told Claude that I would never hold grudges; I had to get on with my life. If I thought about it too much, if I agonised over 'what could have been', I'd have turned myself into knots. It would've destroyed me. As I've said, things happen for a reason, and if you are a good person they are generally for the better. This is the only thought that kept me sane.

We were coming to the end of an era at the Dragons. My good mate, prop Jason Ryles, was heading overseas to play at Catalans. In April it had been announced that Wayne Bennett – the most successful coach in history – would be replacing Nathan Brown at the end of the year.

It had been a hard road for Browny, who was headed to England to coach Huddersfield. He'd had so many great players – champion players – but we didn't put it together as a team. I think we relied on individual talent to come up with certain plays at the crucial time. There wasn't the system in place that we needed, or maybe we weren't mature enough as players. Knowing what I know now, I think if we had a more disciplined, simplistic approach we may have won a title in 2005 or 2006. Hindsight is a wonderful thing.

We couldn't crack into the top four as we edged closer to the finals. I thought we were still a chance to win it, but we had a lot of hard work in front of us. The halves had changed a lot between Jamie Soward, Mat Head, Rangi Chase and Benny Hornby. But I have to admit, the team harmony wasn't the best. Blokes were moving on, Browny was leaving. More people were thinking about themselves ahead of the team.

Leaving my teammates behind was the toughest part of it. I loved all the boys, and we'd been through so much. The good thing was that I was honest with them the whole way. When the time came to tell them, they were understanding. I'd kept a lot of them in the loop. They knew how frustrated and pissed off I was. They were angry for me.

We finished the season in seventh position and came up against eventual premiers Manly in the first week of the finals at Brookvale Oval. They pumped us 38–6.

Instead of celebrating the season with my teammates on one last Mad Monday, I was on a plane to Paris. To a new life, where Claude had already arrived two weeks earlier to find an apartment. I was sad to be leaving, but in some ways I was glad to be going. That was the end of it: the worst year of my life.

THIRTEEN

LE GAZ

'YOU HAVE A VERY pretty face,' said Max Guazzini, the flamboyant owner of Stade Francais, the first time he met me. I can't ever remember Peter Doust saying that to me. From the moment I landed in Paris, ready for the next chapter of my life and career, I knew things were going to be very different.

When I got off the plane after the 29-hour flight from Sydney, having played a game of rugby league just two days earlier, I was greeted by Claude and her mum, Irene. Claude had found us an amazing little apartment in the 16th arrondissement that overlooked the famous River Seine, and we also had glimpses of the Eiffel Tower.

Within 15 minutes of arriving at the flat, Laurent Quaglia, the French agent who did the deal with George, was on the phone saying he would be around to pick me up. He was taking me to meet Max, the French entrepreneur who had taken over the club in the early 1990s because he wanted to bring top-class rugby back to the French capital.

I'd heard stories about Max. How he was an openly proud, gay man – not that such a thing mattered to me – but I knew he was eccentric and had a lot of front. I was concerned about meeting him because he could not speak much English – and I couldn't speak much French at all.

When we arrived at the football offices, there was a cartoon-like statue of a blond footballer out the front, wearing a signature pink Stade Francais jersey. We walked into the building, the heat blazing because it was freezing cold and raining outside. In the corner was an office closed off from the rest where Max was seated.

'This is Mark,' Laurent said in French. 'He is happy to be here.'

Max is a stylish, young-looking bloke, and he spoke a tiny bit of English. 'Hello, Mark,' he said. He was a really nice guy. Then he made the comment in French that I had a pretty face. When Laurent told me, I didn't know what to say! Luckily he told me this in a break in conversation, so I didn't have to reply.

That wasn't the end of my introduction. All I wanted was to go to bed. Instead, I was dressed in a team suit and whisked away to a club function.

It was a relief to see Ewen McKenzie, who introduced me to a few of the players. I was really nervous, because of the language barrier and the fact that I didn't know any of them. It was daunting. I met pretty much all the players but obviously only had conversations with the English-speaking guys, like the South Africans and Argentineans.

Once the dust settled and I'd had a bit of a chance to get around and speak to a few of the guys, I thought it might be an all right night, even though my eyes were hanging out of my head. Then Max got up and spoke. Then he asked me onto the stage and introduced me to the room. Then he asked me to say a few words.

'What do I say?' I asked Simon Taylor, a Scottish international who I was sitting next to. 'Hello,' he replied. Now that I know Simon really well, this was his dry sense of humour on display, which I have to say would make me laugh a lot over the next 20 months. 'Tell them you love them,' he said.

I got up and said I was happy to be here, that I couldn't wait to train with the guys. In truth, I was rattled. Someone translated and everyone clapped.

I'd been looking forward to living in Paris, right in the middle of Europe. I have always enjoyed travelling and had been to Paris three times. When it came to the rugby, however, I have to admit that my excitement was tempered. I knew that I wasn't going to touch the ball much. But that didn't mean I wasn't going to put in as hard as I could. I didn't want them to think I was over there for a holiday. I knew I wasn't there to further my career, but I would always do the best I could by the club. I had never dodged training in my life, and I wasn't about to start.

Stade Francais had won all five games and were undefeated, sitting at the top of the ladder in the French Top 14, which is the name of the domestic league. The club was founded in 1883, and its traditional home is Stade Jean-Bouin – 'the little stadium' – but for the blockbusters they play in the 80,000 seat Stade de France. The club had played in the lower divisions for 50 years or so before Max came along in the early 1990s and turned it into a so-called glamour club.

The plan was to slowly work me up in training until I was ready to play, but after a week they threw me straight in on the wing in a match against Bourgoin-Jallieu, a club based in a city known as the Capital of the French Alps. Christophe Domimici – the Campese of French rugby and Ewen's backs coach – came up to me. 'You're training too good,' he said. 'You're playing.'

What do I remember about my first game of professional rugby? I'll tell you what I remember: entering the dressing-room and seeing a pink shirt waiting for me. A shirt that read 'Pink is Beautiful' in English and in black type on the front, with a thunderbolt down the middle.

The boys told me to put it on – it's what we wear during the warm-up. My first thought: *When my brothers find out about this, they are going to* flog *me.*

Instead, I put my jersey on to warm up. The French boys came up to me straightaway. 'Il n'est pas possible!' they said, waving their hands. Translation: it's not possible. I went up to our South African-born centre, Brian Liebenberg. Was this a gee-up?

He started laughing. 'No, Gaz,' he said. 'You have to wear it.'

I was mostly concerned about it being televised and

broadcast back in Australia, but in the end what choice did I have? So I went out and warmed up in my pink 'Pink is Beautiful' shirt with the thunderbolt down the middle. No, I wasn't at Kogarah no more, unless my jersey had run in the wash!

The team fashion was only the start of my bizarre trip. I said to Brian Liebenberg, 'Mate, can you just tell me where to stand?' I was still very much in league mode, having just played a semifinal two weeks ago. I'd played only one game prior . . . at school. Now I was asking the No.12 where I had to position myself for a professional game of rugby. He was laughing his head off.

He then took full advantage of it. When there was a stoppage, he was telling me what could happen. He'd say, 'Gaz! Gaz! Quick, up here! Up here!' I'd sprint up the field and get into the defensive line for no reason, and he would just laugh and say, 'Get back! Get back!'

I scored a try in the 38th minute, and in the end we ran out as 32–25 winners. There was a lot of European-based media at the game, and also a lot of hype. It was later reported that I'd run around the full-back and scored a great try. I didn't at all – it was a nothing try.

'There are similar principles here but the games are very different,' I said at a press conference after the game. 'Your roles change, so I think your expectations change. My role there early on was to chase a lot of kicks and try to catch them and win possession. I didn't expect to set the world on fire. It was more a matter of getting a feel for the game. It was more a feeling of relief than anything. You feel like you're starting again in a way because you're still learning the rules and different scenarios.'

I didn't get caught up too much in the media, either after that game or during my whole time in France. I would speak to Mum every Sunday, and she would tell me, 'Oh, you're in the paper this week.' At the start I would say, 'Yeah, Mum, I don't even want to know.' And in the end the media coverage I was receiving stopped coming up in conversation.

In the second game, against Montauban at the Stade Jean-Bouin, disaster struck. I went up to catch a bomb, came down and snapped ligaments in my ankle. We won the match 34–16 to remain undefeated, but I was in serious doubt for our opening match of the Heineken Cup, which is the competition held among the top European clubs.

I was meant to miss six weeks, but I came back after two. I pushed it because I wanted to prove my desire to play. As it turned out, it was the worst thing I could have done because my ankle was never the same for the next two years, until I had an operation after the 2010 Grand Final. I made the decision to play, not the club doctors nor specialists, so the fault is all mine.

For the rest of the season, I struggled a bit in wet conditions. My ankle was sore. I managed to play a few good games, but I probably didn't play consistently the way I wanted. I was playing a bit of wing, a bit of centre, but was restricted because of my ankle and the fact that we kicked a hell of a lot, which meant involvement was limited.

When I first arrived in Paris, the media in Australia called me 'Le Gaz'. In one French newspaper, though, they called me 'Star Anonyme' – the 'Anonymous Star'. I'm not entirely sure how the French public perceived me, or if they accepted me, because of the language barrier. To be honest, I didn't really care. One of the best things about my time overseas was pursuing interests off the field. During the season, I really concentrated and put everything into my training, reassuring the guys I was committed. The moment I finished rugby, I was away from it. I was visiting new places, doing different things.

One thing that really surprised me about the club, though, was the lack of emphasis on injury prevention and recovery. This is the number one priority in training methods in the NRL, mainly because of the salary cap. In France, there's no salary cap, and when you are injured and unable to play, the government subsidises your wage through work cover. Therefore, the club is not out of pocket when you're injured like it is in the NRL.

There were some great players over there – athletes, for that matter. Fly half Juan Hernandez, an Argentinean, was one of them. He was the closest thing I've seen to Trent Barrett – his build, his skill set, his kicking game. He was a great player. The same can be said for Sergio Parisse and Juan Manuel Leguizamón.

At Stade Francais you had these great footballers from around the world, who were being paid great money to play here, yet the facilities were something you'd associate with your junior club. Some of the parks we trained at were just recreational parks around Paris. We would train on hockey fields in winter because the rest were covered in snow. I didn't like playing in snow, but training in it was pretty funny. The first season I was there, it was the coldest winter in 12 years. The temperature was consistently minus 12.

The substandard training facilities did not correspond with the extravaganza that Max put on at the Stade de France – 'the big stadium', as everyone called it. They were amazing events, regularly filled to capacity with some 80,000 people. In my first year, the club averaged a crowd of about 72,000 per game.

Again, Max is smart. Once the draw was released, he'd identify the six games that he wants in the big stadium. And then he'll start to market them, offering family packages: kids could come in for only a few euro. A lot of the crowd was all families. Fans would catch the TVG train from the south of France, since most of the other clubs were from that part of the country. The Paris Metro had a station right at the ground. They would come from everywhere because the actual game was only one part of the spectacle. Everyone arrives two hours early, watches the pre-game show, then the game, and then there's a heap of fireworks after the match.

When I first played there, in a game against Clermont, we were warming up on the field and there were motorbikes circling around us in front of a massive crowd. The boys had told me about it, along with the fact that Stade had never lost there. We had a few injuries and I was returning from my crook ankle. We'd won nine in a row, so it was a huge game. Then, when we ran onto the field, the motorbikes were doing flips and jumps, and in the middle of it all was a large troupe of dancing girls.

Max had a different theme for every game. There was a Roman theme, with guys on horseback with swords, like something out of *Gladiator*. On another occasion, I jogged onto the field and there they were: 12 topless girls from the famous Moulin Rouge club. It was minus five degrees, but that didn't seem to matter.

'Did you see that?' I asked Simon.

'Of course I did,' he said in his thick Scottish accent. 'Do you think I'd miss that?'

Max always put on a function afterwards. Moët & Chandon and amazing food all around. One thing I loved about the French rugby culture was that it was compulsory for the away team to attend the home team's function and have some food and a beer or wine with the opposition. It was great, especially for me, as I got to experience all the different cultures within France since the south is very different to the north. It also allowed me to mingle with other players from the different clubs.

Max also loved bringing out a new jumper. I had been there a month when he released one inspired by Andy Warhol. It had all these different faces of the Virgin Mary. They even had to have the design signed off by the Roman Catholic Church. Two other players and I modelled the jersey for Fashion Week in the big Adidas building on the Champs-Élysées.

I was really embarrassed. I kept asking, 'Where do I stand? What do I do? Where do I go?' There was a red carpet and champagne and all the photographers . . . and Fashion TV. It was hilarious. I think I'm probably the only footballer who's done an interview with Fashion TV. *What a wanker!* was my first thought.

I can only say I was thankful that I didn't have to appear in the club's Dieux du Stade (Gods of the Stadium) calendar, the famous nude calendar that Max puts out every year. I did the shoot, but I didn't get in the raw so I didn't make the cut. Or maybe it was my looks. I never asked.

The French culture is so different to the Australian way of life. I think that's why a lot of players struggle when they go over there: to a certain point, they either embrace it or they brush it. If you are polite about it and just say, 'You know, because of my family values I don't want to do the calendar and stuff,' they are all right about it. Actually, they think Australians are all stiffs. Max did, to a certain extent.

But I liked Max; he was a funny man. The concepts that he came up with for his club took things to a level that rugby league could learn a lot from. If you speak to anyone in Europe who knows rugby, they all know Stade Francais. It is the most recognisable brand in the game, a profile which he's built from scratch.

Rugby league could go down a similar path. It certainly opened my eyes to the benefits of privatisation. League players argue about their wages being restricted under a salary cap. If clubs weren't restricted by the NRL in the amount of personal sponsors they could generate for their players, imagine what it would mean for their revenue streams.

If you're a big brand, and you're a big club, you make big money. In Europe, Max released three jerseys every year, and they all sold out. Every one.

One thing I loved about the privatisation of all the French clubs was that there was just as much media interest in the rich presidents of the respective clubs going head to head as there was in the players.

I'll say it again: everything happens for a reason. The life experience I gained in France and what Claude and I became as a couple, meant the contract dispute that forced me to this part of the world was the biggest blessing in disguise. It didn't justify losing the unpaid money, but it made it easier.

During the year, every second we got, Claude and I would travel. I'd ring her and say I had the weekend off, and we would drive for ten hours to Oktoberfest in Germany. Or I'd go down to Morocco and surf. We travelled to Italy, Berlin, Brussels and Munich.

Europe opened my eyes. My priorities changed. Europeans value things differently to us. The Australian dream of owning your own house and having two kids by the time you're 32 works us into the ground and deters us from what's really important – time with family and friends, and broadening your horizons. In Paris, in particular, people just rent apartments, socialise and get on with their lives. I am not saying their philosophy is completely right, but it taught me to have a bit of balance. Yes, be determined, driven and work hard, but don't forget what's important and the things that make you happy. Don't confuse material things for status and fulfilment. It's my personal opinion that we do that a bit in Australia.

There, the drinking culture is very different too. When they do drink, it's not to excess. I used to be very much a binge drinker. Living in Paris, we'd go out at 11pm and drink wine until 3am. We would end up happy, but not stupid. And most drinking is done in restaurants. Again, I'm not saying it's the *right* way to socialise, but I liked it and it was different to what I was used to.

We made a lot of close friends during my time in Paris, I caught up with some of them when I went over for the World Club Challenge with the Dragons in 2011, having jumped on the Eurostar across to Paris. I will always remain indebted to those people who were so welcoming and helpful throughout my time there. They didn't have to be.

When I'd walk along the Champs-Élysées, ex-pats would yell out 'Gaz!' Aussies who had been living in London and were on holidays in France would often come and see me play. They'd introduce themselves after the game, and it was really nice to hear a familiar accent every now and again. But I still felt like I was in another world.

Early on, it had been hard. It was cold. It was strange. I remember one day watching *The Simpsons* in French on television and thinking how weird it all was. But once I became familiar with my surroundings – the shops, training, the language – things improved.

When it came to learning French, I was blessed to have Claude by my side, who helped me with my vocabulary. The only way I could learn the language was to immerse myself in it. I was so frustrated at times. Claude would try to teach me two words a day, and as I learned them the boys at the club would teach me the joining the words. When I was around my teammates, I was learning slang. But when I went to functions, I would struggle a little because there is a formal and informal vocabulary.

French is a very difficult language to learn, because, along with formal and informal words, there are masculine and feminine ones, too. If I'm referring to you informally, I'd say 'tu'. But if I just met you, I would have to say 'vu'. It's a respect thing. If you are speaking to your parents, or your elders, you have to speak a certain way. I would often use the feminine words, because they were the ones Claude taught me, but then I would get to training and try to put them into practice and all the boys would burst out laughing because I said them the feminine way. Oh well, trial and error was still a good way to learn, and the guys appreciated it.

The French always say hello and greet each other. In Paris, if you're late to training you have to come in and shake the hands of every player. But one of the players, Dimitri Szarzewski, would barely speak to me ... for three and a half months. I thought he couldn't speak English. I would try to speak French as much as possible around my teammates. They'd laugh but appreciated that I was trying. Then, one day, he started speaking back to me in English. At first I was angry, but then I realised he was content having me try to speak French in order to help me – that's how a lot of the French are. In the end, I was speaking French, and it's really weird when you have your first dream in a foreign language. One of the boys said that's when you know you've lived in another country for a while.

At the end of the season we finished fourth on the ladder, and then lost to Perpignan in the semifinal. By then, my body was completely spent. I had gone straight from the NRL into the Top 14 season, as well as Heineken Cup matches.

Mum and Dad came over and we travelled some more. From Corsica, all through Nice, Cannes, Monaco and the Amalfi Coast. During my two years over there we pretty much covered all of Western Europe.

Having played two seasons back to back, in two different hemispheres, I needed the break.

In the second year of my two-year deal, I found things to be much easier. There had been talk about me becoming a Wallaby and returning home, something that had been enhanced after meeting with then-Wallabies coach David Nucifora when they had been in Europe on the Spring tour in late 2008. I said at the time I would see how things went, but I was enjoying life too much to think too far ahead.

Then, five matches into the 2009–2010 Top 14 season, Ewen McKenzie was sacked after a poor start. 'We noticed that the coaches' message was no longer really getting through, and we decided to change, in mutual agreement with Ewen McKenzie and Christophe Dominici,' Max said.

I found it hard. Because of the language barrier, I couldn't understand exactly what had happened. I think a few of the senior players had lost faith in him. In any club these days, the senior playing group has a fair bit of power. I felt sorry for Ewen. His hands were tied over there – I could see that. There were politics at the club and it was pretty lonely for him, away from his wife and daughters, who had stayed in Australia.

I actually said to him after his termination that it was a blessing in disguise. He landed a job at the Queensland Reds, and anyone involved in rugby knew they had great depth coming through, a huge junior base to pick from. He returned and won the 2011 Super Rugby title. I was really happy for him.

I was concerned for myself when he left, though. He was one of the main reasons why I went to Stade Francais in the first place. By then, luckily, I felt pretty comfortable playing.

Ewen was replaced by a Frenchman, Jacques Delmas, who was really good to me straightaway. He'd coached Biarritz to the final of the Heineken Cup and won a comp with them, too. He had a fair reputation and said, 'We'll get you the ball as much as possible.' He encouraged me to touch the ball as much as I could and didn't make things too complicated. He played me at full-back a fair bit and simply said, 'When you get the ball, just run. Kick if you have to, but your first instinct should be to just run.' Which stood well with me.

While we didn't reach the finals that season, I was loving life in Paris both on and off the field. I look back now and reflect on the whole experience as one that definitely hap-pened for the better, even if I hadn't wanted to go there in the first place.

France really moved me out of my comfort zone. I went to a country where I didn't speak the language, playing a game that was foreign to me, and to top it off I had a fair bit of pressure. But I believe that's when you discover the real you. You don't have any outside influences and you are not obliged to be someone's ally. It was a great test and a lesson for me, especially mentally.

My whole perspective on life changed after Paris. It gave me time to get rid of grudges, time to take a step back from everything I'd been surrounded with in my life. People said it when I returned to Australia: I was a different person.

FOURTEEN

CHOKE ON THAT

IT WAS JANUARY 2009 when my manager, George, came to Paris and asked me straight out, 'Would you consider coming back?' My answer could not have been any clearer: 'No.'

I had no intention of returning to Australia to play rugby league, and there were two reasons that made it a straightforward decision. First, Claude and I were having a great time living in Europe. It had opened up a new world to both of us and we were enjoying it. More than that, though, I was still bitter about what had happened with my sponsorship contracts. I still hadn't been paid any money. There was still no light at the end of the tunnel. I thought, *Well, what's the point?* For the next year, George would revisit the question randomly – not that he was hammering me with it. I wasn't sure if Peter Doust was asking him the question, either. But my answer was always the same: 'No, George. No way.'

Then one day after I got off the phone with George, Claude asked me, 'Why don't you go back?'

'Because of principle,' I replied.

'So out of principle you will give up what you want to achieve? The only one losing out is you!'

Claude knew this observation wouldn't have made any sense to me 15 months earlier, but living in Europe had taught us a lot of life lessons, and now we – me in particular – had a different thought process.

It was December 2009 when I told George, if the right opportunity came along, I would return to rugby league – and obviously it had to be with the Dragons. I remember saying to him, 'All right, I will. If it can be done, I will.' That started the tricky and delicate negotiations of my returning to Australia.

There was some interest from Newcastle and Manly – they had heard I was thinking about returning to league. Manly's coach at the time, Des Hasler, had spoken with George. I also met with mining magnate Nathan Tinkler, who at that stage hadn't bought the Knights but was a major sponsor.

Nathan was a lovely guy – very down-to-earth. When I returned to Australia, with no deal done yet, I went up to Newcastle to meet him because I wanted to be courteous and give him some due respect and consideration. He had been prepared to give me his. While I listened to what he had to say, I was up front and honest. I was only going to look at other clubs if there wasn't an opportunity to return to the place where it had all started.

'Look guys, I'm flattered,' I basically said to the Knights

and Sea Eagles. 'But the Dragons are my first and foremost preference. I'm going to give them until the eleventh hour to see if they can work everything out with the salary cap, and if it's all fine I'm going there.'

The Dragons and I always got along well, despite what had happened in the past. I would have felt like a dog if I came back and went to another club. My main concern wasn't so much money but the premiership and the thought of finally winning one. We had always copped so much flak about choking – it's such a traditional and proud club. I thought I would be letting myself down if I didn't go back and have a crack. I didn't want to live with the regret of knowing what might have been.

But there were risks. My body was crap. It was in the worst condition of my career, not just because I had an ankle that really needed surgery – although that injury in itself filled me with self-doubt. I'd ask myself, *If I have surgery, am I going to come back as well?* As I've mentioned, the level of training in French rugby doesn't compare favourably to the rigours of life in the NRL. If I came back, I knew I would struggle to feel sharp. I was certainly apprehensive – everyone has reservations in life – but if you don't try to live up to your potential, you'll never know what you're capable of. Australians would rather see a person put their balls on the line and fail than sit back and not have a go.

Around March of that year I talked with Wayne Bennett. He'd had such a massive influence in his first year at the Dragons, taking them to the minor premiership in 2009 before they were bundled out in the finals series with two losses.

I had also kept in contact with a fair few of the boys while I was over in Paris, and I knew the players' work ethic and bond was really strong. Wayne had everyone on the same wavelength. Everyone knew their job. He simplified the game plan for a lot of guys, and that approach was bringing out the best in them. He gave them a few things to concentrate on, and told them not to worry about anything else. If every person did that, they could be a successful team.

Wayne said he was comfortable with my return. I had explained the whole situation surrounding my departure in 2008 before I left for France. He saw that it wasn't a money grab; I wasn't greedy. He knew I had been in a bad situation and why I had to leave. Wayne said he could see where I was coming from.

He had signed on as coach in early 2008, when it was uncertain if I would stay at the Dragons, and I felt I had given him plenty of warning throughout that season to ensure he could plan around my departure. When it came to the possibility of my returning to the club, I spoke to him with the same openness. He wasn't the biggest factor in bringing me home, but he would certainly be the icing on the cake if I did.

After my initial refusals, coming back home just seemed right. I had talked to my family first, then I spoke to Dousty. I spoke to Benny Hornby. I spoke to Benny Creagh. Claude was happy about the prospect of a homecoming. She saw how little involvement I had in rugby, compared to what she'd watched in league, and knew I was frustrated. She knew where I belonged.

My family was obviously ecstatic about the idea. Mum

had been shattered when I went overseas. She loved coming to the football and watching me play. She's been my biggest supporter since I was a kid, taking me to all my games, and until the day I retired she only missed a handful. She'd come to all my State of Origins. She went on my first Kangaroo tour. She went away with me when I played Australian Schoolboys, my try-outs for NSW teams, no matter where they were being held. She had been there through it all and was over the moon about the prospect of me wearing the Red V again.

There was another factor that made us want to come back to Australia. In February, Claude and I returned to get married. All we were hoping for was a sunny day since the reception was to be held at Fort Denison in the middle of Sydney Harbour. It rained the whole day – actually, it absolutely pissed down. It was the most rain Sydney had had in one day in seven years. Good timing! The climate in Paris had prepared us well, though.

It was a fitting moment when we married – we'd been through so much. I said in my wedding speech that when you live overseas as a couple, you are so dependent on one another. When there are no outside influences, it allows you to see your real self. And Claude could see the real me as well. I was ecstatic that we were getting married. We both valued the same things and wanted a family. Honestly, Claude was the main thing that kept me happy throughout all the mess I was going through with my football. She was refreshing, fun to be around, and I hadn't had this much love and respect for a person since I was a kid with my mum. So now that we were tying the knot in front of family and friends who we hadn't seen since we left Australia, it was one of the best days of my life. I couldn't have been happier, which was amazing considering where I had been a year and a half ago.

The following month, however, things went south again. Claude's father, Jean-Pierre, who appeared so healthy at the wedding, was diagnosed with cancer of the mouth, and that made our decision to come home very clear. Stade Francais were great throughout the whole thing. They knew our personal situation and about Claude's dad's illness, and completely understood why we wanted to come home. And they knew my heart belonged to rugby league.

But it wasn't going to be that simple. Wanting to come back and play for the Dragons was one thing. Whether I *could* come back was another. At some stages, the negotiations were strained and my return was touch and go. The Dragons had to juggle the salary cap, and I said to George that I wasn't fussed about the dollars and cents, especially for 2010. I knew I had to be squeezed in under the cap.

I had also made it very clear to George and the club that the deal had to be watertight. I didn't want any third-party agreements, no 'letters of intent', and I wanted my salary paid monthly. I didn't want to go down any other path – why would I after what had happened in the past? The lesson had been learnt.

The Dragons tried to register a contract at $50,000 for the remainder of the 2010 season, but the NRL knocked it back straightaway. The message was clear: There's no way the deal is only that much. It's bullshit. You are hiding money somewhere. They wouldn't register it, even though it was completely above board.

In the end, I signed on for the remainder of that season for $110,000. People have assumed that I came back for a big back-ended deal. I didn't. I was paid $110,000 in 2010. I was paid $250,000 in 2011. And if I'd kept playing I would've been paid $350,000 in 2012 and $400,000 in 2013.

Now that the deal was done, I had this whole visual concept of how things were going to go when I arrived back home. I knew that the first six months were going to be really hard. I thought I was going to cop shit and that I wasn't going to play to my potential.

And I was prepared to hear the criticism that would inevitably come, to be labelled a 'blow-in' and all the rest, because I had come into a winning culture, under a winning coach. All I knew was that I was doing the right thing. I was giving myself the right opportunity, and the body would come good eventually.

We'd arrived back in Australia permanently in early May, and the night I landed, the Dragons were comprehensively beaten by Manly at Brookvale Oval.

I started training with the team's long-time strength and conditioning coach and my good mate Andrew Gray. We had three or four weeks to go before I would make my return to the NRL, and we had a lot of work to do. Since the deal was still not completely signed off, we trained on the quiet.

Funnily enough, we trained right next to Cronulla's home ground of Shark Park. I actually saw the boys a few times as I lifted weights at the Fitness First opposite the leagues club. I was underweight by about six or seven kilograms, which is a lot for a professional footballer. It was solely from the training program in French rugby and the position I was playing, full-back. But if anyone could get me back to the physical level I needed to be in order to play at the top level again, it was Drew. He'd known me throughout my entire career. High-performance manager Jeremy Hickmans, as well as some of the other staff at the club, were also great. I never had any doubt that I could get my body back to where it needed to be to play NRL at the highest level, but it was just a matter of when.

My first session back with the Dragons was a recovery session, playing wheelchair basketball in Wollongong. There were no big speeches. Wayne just said, 'Mark's back.' That's all. I knew there would be no guarantees as far as filling in anyone's spot. I'd have to put myself into a position to play.

I trained with the squad for a few weeks and eventually a 5 July Monday night game against Penrith was slated as my return match. A week before, I finally spoke publicly about coming back to the Dragons. In an interview with *The Daily Telegraph*, I was asked how it would feel to stand in the rooms at Kogarah once again, looking at the white jumper with the Red V. 'Good.' I smiled. 'I've thought about that a lot. You look at your jersey when you put it on . . . and it's a bit better than pink.'

The next day, Wayne spoke at a press conference about

the return of league players from rugby union: 'It says a lot about the product. Their grounding is in rugby league. Mark played all his football in rugby league. The game attracts you, the game gets you. Lote Tuqiri came back, Wendell Sailor, Timana Tahu, Mat Rogers. It says a lot about rugby league and what it gives them. They have done their time in another code, but the grass is not always greener on the other side. Fortunately they have all been young enough to come back, and rugby league has welcomed them back. That is the quality of rugby league as well.'

My comeback match was anything but spectacular. It was wet and cold and the conditions were terrible. I came on in the 26th minute and barely made an impact. I dropped the ball twice in the closing stages of a 12–8 loss to the Panthers, who were second on the ladder behind the Dragons.

I'd always known it was going to be tough, that it wasn't a matter of just walking back into the game. There had been some suggestions that I could've played Origin for NSW if I'd come back earlier, but that was rubbish. I attended the third and final Origin match of that series two nights after my first game and was reminded of how much work I had to do.

As I'd said in a weekly column I had started writing for *The Telegraph*: 'Of course I would like to play Origin for New South Wales again – I just have to learn to catch the ball again!'

I also had to address some criticism that was coming my way from two legends of the game in Australian captain Darren Lockyer and Penrith's skipper at the time, Petero

Civoniceva. They had publicly questioned how the Dragons could've fitted me under the salary cap that year. 'I have
enormous respect for both those guys,' I wrote in my column, 'and it's good to see two of the most senior players in
the game caring about where it's headed. But they can only
question so far. If a player wants to go to a club for less, ultimately it is his decision. As long as you abide by the salary
cap rules, which are black and white, and Ian Schubert signs
off on them, then that's fine.'

To be honest, I was more concerned about making head-
way on the field – because I knew a lot of shit was coming my
way off of it. In my second match back, against South Sydney,
Wayne selected me to come off the bench again. I came on
in the first half and was in the right place at the right time
to race 60 metres and score the match-winner in our 16–13
win. It ensured that we stayed on top of the ladder, where we
had been for much of the season.

It took me about six to eight games to get back into the
groove of rugby league. My body felt like shit. My ankle
injury was also a concern, but I knew if I stuck with it, my
form would eventually come good.

Then we lost the next two matches, against the Gold
Coast and Brisbane, and the familiar old tag started to come
out: 'chokers'. The Roosters clash at the SCG was my first
game in the starting side. My return to right centre had seen
Beau Scott shuffled into the backrow.

After we lost against the Broncos, I knew questions about
my return were coming. Former Parramatta half-back Peter
Sterling was the first to say it on Triple M. 'It's a ripple effect.

They started with Mark Gasnier . . . That pushed Beau Scott into the back of the scrum where he hasn't started for a long time. Which has the effect that somebody misses out in that front six who's done a great job to get them there. But they've always said that the best of Mark Gasnier would be next season. I'm just wondering if they'll have to make a decision as to how they use him.'

It didn't worry me too much, because I knew how we were travelling as a team. I knew I hadn't upset that dynamic. That's the truth. The let-down in form was just due to a bit of fatigue, especially from players who'd endured a long season and played representative footy. We tapered our training because of what the guys learnt the previous year in 2009. They said they'd felt really flat when the semis arrived. In 2010 we were doing things differently, so history didn't repeat itself.

We beat the Roosters the following Sunday at the SCG, my first game with the No.3 on my back, but then lost to Canberra the next week. Even then, I wasn't concerned. I had prepared myself for all the personal criticism. I thought the best thing I could do was train as hard as I could and play my role as best I could without worrying about the fancy stuff, the pretty attacking football, and the boys would see that I was fair dinkum.

The key difference for us was the belief Wayne had instilled into the side. That was the biggest thing I noticed when I arrived back at the Dragons: the demeanour and confidence levels of certain players, not only when they took the field but off it as well. Wayne had made their jobs straightforward. He had broken down our style of play and given each of us simple jobs. Players were confident they could do those fundamental things, and do them well.

We also practised a lot. Muscle memory is such an important thing because when people are fatigued they resort back to old habits, and you have to train those bad habits into good ones. Our team was a bunch of small cogs that turned the big cog. We were being labelled boring and simplistic, but if it got us a premiership, I was sure our fans wouldn't care. The players certainly didn't.

The person who had changed the most under Wayne was Jamie Soward, our five-eighth, and everyone could see it. I got to know Sowie well in 2007 when he first came to the club, because we would carpool to Wollongong for training and games with winger Jason Nightingale. I knew after a few of those hour-long drives that there were few people in the world who loved rugby league as much as Jamie. When he played his 100th match that season, I was proud of him.

For his entire first-grade career, all Sowie ever wanted was for someone to believe in him. The Roosters had let him go midway through 2007. There was always talk about Sowie being small and a liability on defence, but Wayne had helped him become a player who took the field with confidence and trained with confidence, and that wasn't easy considering that he was the Dragons' five-eighth. And, as we all knew by that stage, wearing that jumper brought a whole new level of pressure.

Sowie plays on the right side of the field and, along with the other players on that side, Beau Scott and Jason Nightingale, we were all pretty close. After playing about five or six games together, we had a bit of confidence in one another. We were starting to attack down our side a little bit more. We beat the Knights and then Souths in the final two rounds to claim the minor premiership for the second season in a row.

Heading into the finals, I felt good, like my season was just starting. We easily accounted for Manly in the first week, beating them 28–0 at Kogarah. That game was the best I'd felt all year, and it showed in my best performance of the season to that point. The win meant we had the week off, but I was apprehensive about having the break and losing the momentum I'd developed after stringing some games together. The boys who had played in most of the matches all season, however, appreciated the breather.

As it turned out, we were to meet the Wests Tigers in the preliminary final at ANZ Stadium. I was more nervous before that game – the Grand-Final qualifier – than any other game that year, maybe my career. It was a combination of a few things, like the realisation that the plan we had put in place at the start of the season was coming together. We'd also failed a few times in the past at that finals hurdle. I wasn't concerned about it being the Tigers, who had beaten us in the preliminary final in 2005. The media frequently brought that loss up, but it wasn't in my head at all. I only knew that this was the deepest I'd been into the finals in my career. I had also come home from France and walked into this position. A lot of people went into bat for me from me to be there. I didn't want to let them down.

The match, as those who saw it will remember, was as close as it gets. Played before 72,000 people, every play was

tight. The Tigers had led 12–6 at the break, but we had levelled, thanks to a Jason Nightingale try, and then Sowie
landed a field goal from 32 metres out with six minutes to
play, and we held on to win.

The interesting part about reaching the Grand Final was
that we would be playing the Roosters, who had become the
Cinderella story of the season. They had finished woodenspooners the season before, but under new coach Brian
Smith, and with five-eighth Todd Carney playing so well that
he won the Dally M award as the best player in the competition after a year out of the game, they had reached the Grand
Final.

The Roosters also featured a player I knew well: Jason
Ryles, the best man at my wedding and a long-time Dragons teammate before he left to have a stint with Catalans in
the UK Super League. We spoke briefly early in the week,
about Grand Final week and life in general, but that was it.
Claude and I, and Rylesy and his wife, Alana, knew Sunday
was going to be a real good day for one couple, and not so
great for the other.

What do I remember about Grand Final week? Everything.

I'd spoken to the great players over the years, blokes like
Andrew Johns in rep teams, who had told me how incredible the week was. There is something on every day, a crowd
buzzing at every training session. Wayne gave us a good tip:
'Don't ever feel like Grand Final week's a burden. It's one of

the best weeks of your life, and when you're tired or you've got to do an extra promo, just soak it up.'

The day after the Tigers game, the Sydney-based players all did recovery at Cronulla and afterwards headed to my house to get measured up for suits. We ate bacon and egg rolls and chatted. I remember looking at Jamie Soward and he said to me, 'Mate, we're in the *Grand Final*.' Sowie was pumped – everyone was – but we all showed that emotion and excitement in our own way. I don't think it had fully sunk in yet.

We took Wayne's advice and soaked up every moment of that week, and there were no nerves or tension. Before we knew it, it was game day. I remember running onto the field, and the atmosphere was unbelievable. It was like my debut in State of Origin in 2004, except there was red and white everywhere instead of blue. Then we got off to a great start when I scored after just six minutes. Sowie had put in the perfect kick for me to grab and put down just before the dead-ball line.

The play wasn't a fluke. Over the last five weeks of the competition, Sowie had been trying to get me some early ball. Opposition teams were really rushing up on me, flying out of line to shut me down. I'd said to Jamie, 'When you've got the ball and you've got a bit of time, if you fake to run it, just look and put a little kick in behind and we could score.' Sowie's kicking game is second to none; he can put it on a ten-cent piece. We were actually going to try that on the next play, but Sowie got the ball a little bit earlier from an off-load from winger Brett Morris, and then he saw me pointing out wide and placed in a perfect kick.

But then we made a lot of uncharacteristic errors and

invited the Roosters into the match. Their captain, Braith Anasta, scored a controversial try, but some decisions had gone our way as well, with Brett being allowed to play on after going into touch. At half-time, the Roosters led 8–6.

But we weren't panicking. We knew we'd played terribly – couldn't have played any worse, in fact. Wayne, the most successful coach in the history of the game, winner of six Grand Finals, knew exactly what to say: 'Look, you're just making uncharacteristic errors. You don't look yourselves. So just forget about the first half, treat this like you're starting the game again, in the same way you started the other 28 games to get here, and we'll be fine.'

That's all he said. No ranting and raving.

In the first set of six in the second half, we drove down field 50 metres, put in a kick and never really looked back. When Jason Nightingale scored an amazing try using great hands with 20 minutes to go, I knew we had done it. It was such an amazing feeling to know we had the game wrapped up with time on the clock. We won 38–8.

When the full-time siren sounded, after the wild celebrations of winning the premiership, one of the first things I did was go over and speak to Jason Ryles. I shook his hand. 'Mate, I'm not going to sit here and try and make it better,' I said, 'because I don't know what it feels like. But we'll have a beer later in the week.' And we did just that.

The lap of honour was surreal. The look on people's faces made me realise that, while it meant so much personally, it meant everything to the supporters. The years of getting bagged by everyone were finally over, and they had five months to gloat about it – and the ones I'd run into on the street later definitely did.

Then we arrived back in the dressing-room. Wayne didn't say too much. It wasn't a big speech, basically congratulations and that it was all of our hard work that had allowed us to arrive at this moment. All those tough moments throughout our season and careers had paid off. Then he dangled out this piece of fishing line: 'It's even harder to go back to back.' Just to remind us what we had to do next year if we wanted to win consecutive premierships.

To be honest, I did feel like a bit of a blow-in. I had played twelve games, and I hadn't done the pre-season training with this side. That's when you become part of a team, when you earn your stripes. It says a lot about your character during the off-season when you go through that trial by fire. And I had missed it. I had reservations about letting all my emotions out for that reason.

I don't think the others considered me a blow-in. Those who had played with me my whole career knew that I was a decent trainer. I think they knew what sort of character I was. So many people had gone into bat to help me get here mid-season, people like Peter Doust and Wayne and the other players. There were pretty emotional scenes. Our hooker, Dean Young, was in tears. So was his father, Craig, who is an icon at the club. He had been captain in 1979 when St George last won a premiership. Benny Hornby was crying too. I'm probably not the most emotional person in the world – I don't think I've cried since I was about six years old – so I held my emotions in check.

I'm just like my dad. You feel the same emotions, but everyone has different ways of showing it. For me, this premiership was about self-satisfaction and contentment. Without sounding weird, I didn't feel like jumping out of my skin – I just felt at peace with myself.

After a while, Wayne was really good about letting all the players' families into the dressing-room to share in the moment. Mum and Dad. My three brothers. Claude. They had watched everything that had happened over my career, having seen me leave for France in 2008 and wondering if I would play rugby league again. As far as they were concerned, karma had prevailed.

I was especially happy for Mum. As I've mentioned, when it came to my footy, she ran the show. I'm glad as much as anything that she didn't have to leave ANZ Stadium that night with anything less than a Grand Final victory.

Throughout your whole career, you think that when you win a premiership you're going to party for a solid week. You're not going to sleep. We did celebrate – don't get me wrong – but nothing like you might think. The scenes back at Kogarah that night – at the ground where I had played so much of my footy – were incredible. Fans were crying and standing in the rain to celebrate with us. Then we did the parade in Wollongong the following day. We had a few drinks that week and were a little bit dusty. The week is hectic because you are doing Grand Final photos and memorabilia signings. Your phone is ringing off the hook.

The following Monday is when our accomplishment really hit me. For years I had been conditioned, heading into another off-season, to think, *Oh, we stuffed up again.* Not this year. Even now it doesn't come rushing back and overwhelm me with emotion whenever I think about it. I am just content and feel like I can move on a happy man.

FIFTEEN

THE GAME TODAY

FINALLY WINNING A PREMIERSHIP had capped the biggest and most exhausting year of my life. Claude and I had gone through so many highs and lows over the past few years, but 2010 turned out to be the biggest roller-coaster of them all.

The Grand Final win had been significant in terms of footy, but there are more important things than that – believe it or not. We got married in February and in September Claude fell pregnant. The Dragons won the comp in October, but then tragedy struck in November: Claude's dad, Jean-Pierre, lost his fight with cancer and sadly passed away. It was a big hit, particularly for Claude and her family. Death is an extraordinarily difficult thing to deal with, and seeing what Jean-Pierre went through really makes a lot of things I am talking about in this book – footy, contract difficulties, the pursuit of a premiership – irrelevant. But you do your best to manage, and that's all we could do.

I think I've shown that I've always had a bit of perspective when it comes to life and football and where the two meet, even before I came into first grade. Football has to be enjoyable – not that it always was for me – but it also taught me valuable lessons in life. Many people say I was a different person when I came back from France, and I guess I was as far as my thought processes and what I valued outside of the game, but morally and ethically I was still the same person.

France gave me a new perspective on our domestic game. I noticed that some things within rugby league had changed. For instance, I heard plenty of players comment that the game is no longer fun. I think they mean that league is very structured now, and a lot of game plans are basically built around waiting for your opponent to crack rather than you inflicting blows. A lot of plays and strategies are based on risk assessment, not necessarily instinct. Add in coaches who are becoming more controlling than ever since they don't want any extra attention or added pressure on the playing group, and you can see why some people think the game has become a bit boring, from a player's perspective. This is obviously not the case at all clubs but, in speaking with a lot of people when I arrived home, this was the concern of many more players than I thought there would be.

My belief is that you make of the game what you want. Obviously, if you take risks on the field, you will be held accountable. Off the field, life balance is so important to a footballer, just as it is to people in the traditional workforce.

In fact, it's probably more problematic for a footballer to maintain balance since they have people wherever they go wanting to talk about their team's form or an upcoming game or voice their opinion on something. That's fine – a lot of players are happy to have a chinwag – but too much football too much of the time can wear some people down. And I think once coaches know your work ethic and personality, and know you are not getting too far ahead of yourself, then you will get a lot more leeway from them – and the group for that matter.

Fans I speak to often express how they would like to see a bit more flair in the game, along with some fun, like post-try celebrations. Not since my mate Mark 'Piggy' Riddell jumped the fence at WIN Stadium and clapped himself have I seen a post-try celebration. I believe this is because coaches don't like any extra attention or to provide any additional motivation for the opposition. As an ex-player, I can understand that view. But now, as a commentator and a fan, I hope they can find a happy medium, because kids absolutely thrive on a bit of theatre.

I remember when I first came into grade and Nathan Blacklock and Anthony Mundine were doing backflips. It was all the kids wanted to talk about. The wrestle in the tackle is the main thing on fans' lips now, in terms of the spectacle of the game. I remember speaking with Nathan Brown about it back in 2003 when Ricky Stuart had mastered the technique of getting three to four players in on every tackle, allowing them to slow down the ruck and then play the aggressive up-and-in style defence.

We were talking back then about how something had to give, otherwise the game would lose a bit of its appeal. I didn't think I would still be having this same conversation with Wayne Bennett in 2010. I don't have so much of a concern for the wrestle these days, just the third man into the tackle. I hate seeing that person spear in at the legs. If the ball-carrier is good enough to stay standing in a two- or three-man tackle, then that person should be rewarded with a quick play-the-ball.

The formation of the independent commission has been a great thing for the future of rugby league. It is a huge step forward for the NRL, mainly because it gets rid of the past and their alliances from the Super League and ARL days. I have no doubt the commission will maximise revenue potential, but I also hope they will share it evenly with the clubs and players so the game can grow together and everyone is happy to promote a sport we are all passionate about.

For me, the most important issue in today's game is getting the junior structure right, from under-7s through first grade. We are up against it with competition from other popular sports, like soccer under-7s to under-11s, and 90 per cent of the reason for opting against rugby league, when you speak to parents, is the contact associated with the game. I know we have implemented some rule changes to limit that contact, but why don't we get on board with Oztag or a similar association?

In other words, Oztag could replace league from say under-7s and under-10s. Oztag draws great numbers and nothing needs to change other than that they would now come under the commission's banner and the sport would become a stepping stone to limiting the contact in league. At least that way we don't risk losing league-loving kids to soccer. Either way, whatever the commission implements, it needs to be the highest of priorities – without these kids we do not have a future product.

I think this season is shaping up as one of the most defining years in rugby league. With the independent commission now in place and the renewal of the TV rights deal, we have an amazing platform for our future. Where we end up is in the commission's hands.

SIXTEEN

THE END

It was only a few weeks after the Grand Final when I caught up with my manager, George, for dinner.

'I think next year will be my last,' I said.

'We'll just see how you go,' George replied. 'We'll talk about it later.'

I hadn't made a clear-cut decision to retire after we'd won the premiership, but I think those close to me knew I was leaning that way. Claude certainly did. I had been talking to her about my post-football life for so long – almost as long as we had known each other. Much of that speculation was because of the contract frustrations that forced me to move to French rugby.

Some thought I might have walked away from the game for good over the contract disputes, but I was always going to play somewhere. By that age I was a bit smarter and realised that there were a lot of opportunities to earn some good income.

But when we won the comp, I'd obviously ticked the big box that had been vacant for a long time. My main thinking was: *Well, I'll play next year because I know my body will be better. I know I'll play better football. I'll play like I did when I was a kid. I'll just enjoy it.* But, most of all, I knew I had to play one more year to confirm to myself that I did want to retire.

My decision was closely guarded. Claude, the family, George and Dragons Chief Executive, Peter Doust, were the only ones who knew about my pending retirement at the start of the season. It hadn't been confirmed or announced, but the club had to know what I was thinking. What nailed it for me came in the form of our firstborn child, Kalani, on 1 June 2011. The circumstances surrounding his birth weren't all that simple.

My form had stayed solid over the first few months of our premiership defence, and it was enough to warrant selection in the NSW side for the first State of Origin match at Suncorp Stadium. I was very happy to be back playing my first Origin series since returning from France.

My old mate Ricky Stuart had come back as the Blues coach, and he was determined to end Queensland's five-year domination of the series. I had played in the losing NSW side against the Maroons in the final match of the 2006 series, when Darren Lockyer had snatched victory in the dying minutes. That loss hurt me as much as any other at representative level. It would've been great to reverse it in my final season.

The only hitch was that Claudine was due to give birth six days after Origin I. Walking away from a team, before a big game, is something plenty of fathers have had to decide over the years. For me, it was the easiest call in the world: of course I would walk away to be with Claude and the baby. And I still would today, regardless of my job.

Ricky was fine about my potential withdrawal from the side. It's childbirth. Every coach is sweet with it. Yes, we're all caught up in this rugby league world – we're passionate about it; we love it – but your family is your family. When footy goes, it's the one thing that will always be there. I never even thought of staying in camp if Claude went into labour. As I told *The Daily Telegraph* on the first day of camp, 'It's thirty-eight weeks tomorrow and the obstetrician says the baby could come at any time. The baby definitely takes priority. Football is a very important thing in my life, but you can't go past this. I've been waiting for this day for a while now. I'll be a very proud man. I've always wanted to be a father. I just didn't know when it would happen.'

In the end, the call didn't have to be made. We narrowly lost the first Origin game, meaning we had to win in Sydney to keep the series alive, and then I backed up against the Wests Tigers two nights later. We won. Still no baby.

The following Tuesday, the baby *still* hadn't come, so we went to see the obstetrician. She said that the child was thereabouts, but he might take a while. She asked if we wanted to induce the baby, because I was going into camp for Origin II the following week. I didn't care. I told Claude not to base her decision around my football. But in the end she decided not to induce because she was determined that she wanted a natural birth, without any drugs.

The next day, around 4 pm, we were walking around the esplanade at Cronulla Beach when Claude felt something. About three minutes later, she felt another contraction.

'I think we should head home,' I suggested.

'No, we'll be all right,' Claude said.

Then the contractions became more persistent. Claude is pretty tough, but then a few hours later we had no choice. We arrived at St George Private Hospital at 6.45 pm and Claude was already dilated five centimetres. Kalani Jean Gasnier was born at 11.47 that night.

I've liked the name 'Kalani' since I was a kid because of one of my favourite surfers, the great Hawaiian Kalani Rob. I know a few girls called Kalani, but I had never heard of a boy by that name. We wanted his middle name to be Jean, in honour of Claude's dad. And John is my father's name, but we decided to spell it the French way. We would have loved Jean-Pierre to have seen little Kalani. It was strangely fitting because our son had a pretty big resemblance to Claude's father, and he arrived not long after Jean-Pierre's passing.

When a woman gives birth, you have a new-found respect for her. Child birth is an amazing experience, and the toughness women show makes footy players look like whimps! I was amazed. I rang my brothers, and each of them said the same thing: 'I told you it was special.' That night, Claude and I didn't sleep. We just stood over the top of Kalani, staring at him, smiling. The next day, we had all the family come in – and then the reality of footy brought me back down to earth.

On that Friday, two days after Kalani was born, I left the hospital and went to Parramatta Stadium to meet the Eels. We had a couple of injuries and Wayne needed me to play. I'd been at the hospital for the birth and had barely slept for two days. Then I ran out for a game of footy . . . The game was locked at 14–all after normal time. It went all the way through to the end of golden-point extra time, so the result was a draw. I was spent. I remember being in the dressing-room afterwards and thinking, *Get me to bed*.

When you have a baby, you run on pure adrenaline and joy. Claude and I had both wanted a family. We spoke openly about having a child in our second year in France. Then we decided to wait until we could have it in an Australian hospital.

Fatherhood has had a massive effect on my life. It changed my whole perspective. Priorities changed. As Claude would say, I'm a really protective father. Instead of having a coffee with the boys after training, I was rushing home because I missed him.

The next month wasn't easy, though. We went through a tough period because I was playing through the Origin series, and Kalani had really bad silent reflux. Actually, for the first five and a half months he barely slept. Thank God for coffee! During that period, I realised exactly what my own mum and dad must have gone through raising four boys. Parenting is special, and it's not until you have your own children that you realise what your mum and dad sacrificed for you.

Fatherhood confirmed my decision to retire and suggested that there was life after football. Not to be disrespectful to rugby league in any way, but fatherhood and working outside the game was something I had been thinking about in the three years leading up to my retirement and having Kalani. I've always been curious and excited about the business world, and luckily I had some opportunities that I wanted to pursue, both in the corporate world and in the media.

I'd told Claude that I didn't want to play well into my thirties. She didn't believe me at first when we came back from France and I said, 'Look, I only want to play two more years.'

'Bullshit,' she laughed. I maintained that if we won a comp I would walk away.

On 14 July I sat next to Peter Doust at the St George Leagues Club for one last press conference, announcing that I would retire at the end of the 2011 season. 'I've known for a while,' I said. 'While it may come as a shock to a lot of you guys, it's not for me. I knew the other night would be my last Origin; I knew that this Monday would be my last game at Kogarah.'

The NSW side had lost the deciding match of the Origin series, after we had played so well to win game two in Sydney, thanks to a late try from Anthony Minichiello, who had been recalled to the side after several years. Mini and I had come so far since that 2004 series – it's funny how things pan out.

My announcement came as a bit of a shock to the players. I think those who knew me well weren't surprised. I spoke to a few of the boys on the way home from the World Club Challenge, which we had won against Wigan in England in February, and I hinted that this season would be my last. Like Claude, they all thought it was bullshit. I don't think they realised how much and how long I'd actually been turning it over in my mind. They probably thought, *Maybe he's just thinking about it.* Or, more to the point, *He's just talking shit.* I had known all along. I'd told Dousty and George, 'Look, I'm telling you out of respect, so do the right thing by me and don't tell anyone.' When Steve Price was appointed as the man to take over from Wayne in 2012, I told him too so that they could manage the cap. I didn't want anyone to know just yet since I had to work out, once I told Wayne, the best time to announce it so that it wouldn't disrupt our season too much. They're a good, trustworthy bunch at the Dragons. That's what makes them so close.

I still get asked a lot why I retired. My answer: mentally, I'd just had enough. Rugby league was something that excited me for so long, but priorities had changed and I was ready to move on. I didn't want to kid myself, and with the salary cap the way it is you can't afford to be only 70 or 80 per cent committed.

I had always said I wanted to finish on my own terms. I never wanted someone tapping me on the shoulder or a behind-the-scenes coup to push me out. I would have hated that, and I think it would have left a bitter taste in my mouth about my career. I know a lot of players who want to play until they're told that's enough. That just wasn't me. Physically, I think I could've easily played another two years, which is ironic given how much footy I missed over the course of my career with injury.

The decision cost me a significant amount of money, but what's better? To retire happily or have full pockets and not play good footy, where everyone thinks, *hurry up and retire*? I would've been going through the motions. I would've only been good for about eight games. I had achieved what I wanted to in my career and it was time to move on. I didn't want to get greedy.

The fact that I had two years to run on my deal confused a lot of people about my motives. Although I'd signed to come back for four years, I did say to George that I probably wouldn't go that far.

I didn't get involved with the duration of the conract because that's between George and the club. Obviously, managers do the best thing by you, and they go for security.

Soon after the announcement, I was criticised for finishing early. Some people felt the decision to leave early should have been made clearer sooner, because the Dragons had been forced to shed two premiership-winning forwards in Neville Costigan and Jeremy Smith. It annoys me because what was I meant to do about it? And I don't mean that in a selfish way. If the club offers me a deal and wants to sign me for a certain amount of time, what should I say? The club and those particular players were the ones who ultimately made the call. At the end of the day, the salary cap is managed by the coach and the chief executive officer – not me.

Long after my last game, during my first off-season of retirement, there were conspiracy theories about my future.

I was apparently headed to the Knights, or to the Reds where Ewen McKenzie, who I had played under at Stade Francais, has had so much success. Some asked Claude if we were going back to France to play.

Everyone's going to throw in their two bob's worth, but that's one thing I've learned from rugby league and life in general: run with it, because ultimately you know the truth and it will always come out eventually. What people don't know is that I have signed an agreement with the Dragons that I will not play for another club anyway!

For much of that 2011 season we had looked like a team that was listening to the words Wayne had delivered in the dressing-room after we had won the Grand Final. There was a great belief in our club that we could become the first team since Wayne's Broncos sides in 1992 and 1993 to win consecutive premierships. But injuries and the fact that so many of our players had featured in the Origin series took their toll. By the time the finals came around, we had finished fifth on the competition ladder. In the history of the game, very few teams have won from outside the top four.

We lost in the first week of the finals to the Wests Tigers, setting up a semifinal against Brisbane at Suncorp Stadium. It was always going to be a big match for a couple of reasons. Wayne was coaching against his former side, the team where he had won six premierships before leaving to come to the Dragons. Now he was coaching his last few matches for the Dragons, having agreed to join the Knights for four years after Nathan Tinkler had taken ownership of the club.

It was also Darren Lockyer's last season, and he was walking the same tightrope as me, heading into every game like it was his last.

What ensued was one of the tightest and hardest fought games of my career. We had been behind for most of the game before full-back Darius Boyd scored just before half-time, and Jamie Soward kicked a tough sideline conversion to put the game into golden-point extra time.

I thought we were going to win it. I genuinely did. I thought that was going to suit us. Then, when the Broncos had their first set of six, Locky kicked the worst looking field goal I have seen to win the match – and that was it, literally.

My career was finished.

Most fans said, 'Oh, you must be disappointed, that's the last game you'll ever play in league.' But I wasn't. I put the shoe on the other foot. That could have been us last year against Wests Tigers, but we won that match and then we went on to win the comp. I honestly believe that if we had won that match against the Broncos we would've won the competition.

Locky had suffered a fractured eye socket earlier in the game. If he had stayed fit, they might have beaten eventual premiers Manly the following week and then won the premiership.

I've heard of players suffering from depression or struggling to cope with the fact that they have retired. There is no longer another game of football next weekend, no more camaraderie with their peers. Claude had warned me about how mundane the nine-to-five lifestyle can be.

But, since retiring, I have taken up a job with Fox Sports as a commentator. I have also worked in business development and on a senior management team, gaining as much experience in running a business as I can. Hopefully one day I can run my own company. I'm on Nova FM every Friday and am still the corporate ambassador for the Dragons. Throw in the running of my own foundation and life is pretty busy.

The Gasnier Foundation is something my wife and I set up after Claude's dad, Jean Pierre, passed away with mouth, oesophageal and liver cancer. My mum, Janene, was also affected by the disease, along with my sister-in-law, Tina, with melanoma. We are trying to raise $3.5 million so St George Hospital can buy a PET scanner to help the early detection of cancer since there isn't one in the public system between the airport and Canberra, and that's a huge area! We have raised $510,000 to date and hope to reach the target sooner rather than later.

With all this stuff going on, and obviously the most important thing in my life, my family, I haven't really thought about football too much. I believe retiring on my own terms put me in a great frame of mind for life after football. I am content and happy, not only with my past but the prospect of my future as well.

SEVENTEEN

WHAT OTHERS SAY

Janene and John Gasnier, parents
Janene: Mark was born 19 July 1981 at the Royal Hospital for Women in Paddington, New South Wales – our fourth son and brother to Gavin, Brent and Dean. Mark was running at nine months. He was a very talkative toddler, quite cheeky at times, and he learnt a lot from his brothers. Mark started playing rugby league at four-and-a-half years old and loved it. He had watched his three brothers play for the past four years, and he always wanted to do what his brothers were doing. He really looked up to his eldest brother, Gavin, who was also a very good footy player.

    John: In the school holidays, to give Janene a rest, we would go camping in Sofala, near Bathurst. We went there for about five years in a row, in September – before it got too hot in the bush – because of the snakes. We used to camp on the river. We would get the floats and float down the rapids. We'd do a bit of gold panning. They loved it.

As a player, Mark stood out from the time he was a little boy. He had to stay out of football for 12 months because he had growing pains – his bones were growing quickly. It nearly broke his heart. From an early age he'd always resist tackles; he could always step out of where they were tackling. He always had that sidestep. They would pass it to Mark and off he went, that was basically it.

Janene: Mark was a natural. In Mini League, he had a lot of fun. As soon as he had the ball, he was away. Not many could catch him. As he got older, he got better and better, and when he wasn't playing footy he was on the train to Cronulla with his mate Steve Hinton to surf for hours. Although Mark loved his footy, he didn't take it all that seriously. It was fun. I remember a game at Henson Park when Mark forgot his footy gear and boots. It didn't worry him – he just borrowed someone else's who had already played. Mark progressed through the rep teams. When he was 11, he represented New South Wales in the under-12s schoolboys in Darwin. After this, we were approached by player managers. I was stunned. I couldn't believe they were interested in an 11-year-old. At 17, Mark signed with George Mimis and he told us Mark would be a superstar. We had no concept of that at all.

John: It's very rare to find a footballer who can step off both feet and just leave you standing. I knew he'd go to first grade because I had him in the SG Ball when I was the head trainer. Then he played Jersey Flegg, and then they had to pick him in reserve grade. He was under [coach and former

Dragons full-back] Mick Potter then, and you could just see where it was heading. And then he went into first grade, making his debut against Newcastle. I was a strapper at the Dragons – I still am – and I was up there for the game.

Janene: We were both there. When the game finished, I had run the mobile phone flat. I drove out of the ground and straight over the median strip outside the stadium. I was in another world. When we got to the hotel where we were staying, I phoned everyone to tell them that Mark had played first grade. John was cranky. 'You know I'm in bed!' he was saying. And I said, 'Well, listen! My son's just made first-grade football and I have to tell everyone.' So I woke everyone up and told anyone who didn't know . . . most of them had seen it on TV anyway.

John: We bought about $45 worth of papers the next morning. Newspapers everywhere . . .

Janene: Our four boys have all achieved highly in their different fields, but it makes you so proud to see that Mark has never ever been a big-head. At no stage has he been arrogant about his ability, and he has always been a very loving, affectionate and loyal son.

John: Reg was the same. He was never a big-head. Mark was often compared to Reg, but it was a different ballgame. It was the old bash-and-barge when Reg was playing. When you're involved in it you can see the difference between the old days and the new days. I think Mark had a similar running style. Reggie used to run with his head up and they would tell him, 'You'd better get your head down because you'll get it knocked off.' Some of them did. He was a sitting duck.

Janene: We were both there in Newcastle. It was a very memorable event: shock, excitement, nerves and oh-so-so proud of our son. We both had tears in our eyes. Because I had run my mobile phone battery flat and still had a lot of calls to make, I had to wake the manager to turn the phone on in the room. He wasn't happy. I said to him, 'It's not every day your 17-year-old son makes first grade. We called everyone, but most had experienced it on TV. After he made his debut, there were only a handful of times I missed attending games; whenever he played in New Zealand and a couple of games in Brisbane.

John: On one occasion, at a Parramatta game, Janene donged a bloke on the head with an empty Coke bottle.

Janene: As a mother, you hear a lot of good and bad comments about your son at football games, and some really upset you. At times I reacted. One time, we were at Parramatta Stadium and the Dragons were losing. Nathan Brown was waterboy, so it was a while ago. Andrew Farrar was the coach, and his mum and dad were sitting behind me. A guy who appeared a few chops short of a barbie was sitting in front of me, just bagging everyone. I mean, everyone – even the cheer girls. Mark was tackled and didn't get up. I was concerned. Next minute, he yells, 'Get up, you fairy!' That was it. I hit him on the head with an empty Coke bottle and told him to shut his mouth. Andrew's parents said they wanted to do that, too. That guy was a nightmare.

John: He turned around to me and went, 'Your missus has got more fire in her than that whole Dragons team!'

Janene: When Mark left so abruptly to go to France, it left a giant hole in our hearts. Although we knew and understood the reasons, it was hard to take. We accepted it and got on with it. I would get up at all hours and watch his games live on Eurosport. But I didn't enjoy that rugby game. I still watched the Dragons and would tell Mark the score and how they played. The best thing that came out of France for John and me was our wonderful trip to Paris and other parts of Europe. Mark and Claudine made us so welcome. They lived in the heart of Paris, about a ten-minute's walk from the Eiffel Tower. It was just magic.

John: I would never say anything to the Dragons fans, because I wouldn't have a job. Luckily, Mark hasn't got his mum's temper. He's very much like me.

Janene: Winning the Grand Final, after everything he had been through, was something special. The seats we were allocated were right near the tunnel and about eight rows back. There was a big girl on security and she wouldn't let me down to the fence as they did their lap of honour. Mostly all of the fans had gone over the fence and she said, 'No, you can't go down there.' I said, 'Listen. All I want to do is just be there to cheer.' No. She wouldn't let me. So I just climbed over.

John: We got into the dressing-room because Wayne Bennett said, 'Bring the parents in.' It was fantastic.

Janene: It was very emotional. When we all came back to Kogarah Oval, it was even more emotional. Because of where we had all come from to get there.

Gavin Gasnier, brother

He was a smart-arse, but he had a lot of encouragement from his three brothers. Mum had concerns about a three-year-old kid getting around, sticking his finger up, but he had a fair bit of coaching. He also didn't like work that much. We would mow lawns with Dad, and while we were doing all the work, Mark would be getting cake and cordial off the old lady whose lawn we were working on. He also had some bad haircuts. For one of them, he had his whole head shaved but still had four inches of fringe at the front. It was probably the trend back then.

We did a lot of stuff together. Mark was dragged around by the three of us wherever we went. We built a skateboard ramp at the end of our cul-de-sac, which was about six-foot high. Mark had a three-wheeler that kids get around on. We'd drag him up the hill and let him go. He would fly up this skateboard ramp, go up in the air, come back down and land it. We got Mum and showed her. She wasn't happy.

Early on into his career, when he was about 19, he was questioning if professional football was what he wanted to do. He asked me how I felt when I gave the game away, when I quit St George. I knew that he would listen to what I had to say. I never knew that he took comfort from that. That if it hadn't worked out in footy he could find a life away from it. I walked away because I wasn't happy. The only time I regretted that was when he started coming through. Because we could've played together.

Playing for that club, with that surname, wasn't anywhere near as tough for me as it was for Mark. At the age of about

15, I moved from the centre position into the forwards. So there weren't those comparisons. When I played under-17s for New South Wales against Queensland, we were warming up in the fields next to the Sydney Football Stadium. Someone came up and asked, 'Which one is Gasnier?' People wanted to know which one was 'the Gasnier'. But I ended up playing at second-row or prop. Mark was in the same position as Reg. You were always aware that you were more than likely going to be looked at because of the surname.

In the end, Mark learnt to deal with the mention of the surname. It was annoying for him at the start. What Reg did, when he did it, was much different to the modern-day footballer. As players, people would compare them, but they were different. By the time he arrived back from France, he'd learnt to ignore it.

He had plenty of ups and downs, and it was often frustrating for us because people didn't know the truth. When he went to France, it was because he had to. It was something that he didn't really want to do. He wasn't being paid half his wage. To have people say he was going for the money, it was hard to bite your tongue. I told Mark that I had seen plenty of players during my time show loyalty towards the club, but that loyalty didn't always come back. You could never tell people the real truth, because he was chasing the money owed to him, and still is.

When he returned, and finally won the premiership, we were all very happy – even though he came into it halfway through the season. When he came back from France, he was much lighter. Then he strung together some good games and won the premiership that he'd come back for. When we were back at Kogarah later that night, there was a lot of relief for the club and Mark. They had been premiership contenders for so long, and to finally win it. I'm sure that's why he retired early.

Rugby league was never his life. The two of us spoke about it a couple of times: while it's a big part of your life, it's only a game. There is more to life than footy. When he was questioning at that young age what he wanted to do, I told him footy is great and it can provide for your family, but if you are unhappy doing it, it's not worth doing. I thought if he had that frame of mind about his footy, he would perform better. You talk to any player, if they are relaxed, they play better.

Looking back, I can remember so much of his career. I can't remember the game, but he scored a try against Parramatta at Kogarah that was special. When he was picked for Australia, I had a tear in my eye. My wife was angry: 'You wouldn't cry when your kids were born, but you did when your brother was picked for Australia.'

It wasn't a fake cry, like Mark was known for as a kid.

Brent Gasnier, brother

As a kid, he was a smart-arse. He would stir Dean up – a lot. Dean would want to kill him most of the time, and Gavin and I would have to stand up for him. He would stir us up, but whenever it came to any retaliation he would do the biggest fake cry. He was the master of the fake cry. Mum or Dad would come to his rescue, and he would be smiling at us from behind their backs.

He loved surfing because it was an outlet for him. He watched more movies about surfing and snowboarding than sitting down to watch a game of football. But football was what he was good at. When he was nine or ten years old, he'd score five or six tries a game. He always had good speed. He'd run around sides. We would put shit on him as a young fella because his older brothers played in the forwards. We'd say to him he should have a go and run through the middle. He doesn't know what it's like to be a pig. That's why his career went longer than ours.

It meant a lot when he played first grade – to the whole family. Our family's life was football. Winning the premiership was a proud moment for all of us, even though it was a little bit short-lived because he wasn't there for the entire season. And while he had many highs and lows, he managed it all himself. He never cried on anyone's shoulder. Whatever holes he dug for himself, he managed to fill back in. He learnt along the way that anything he did was under the microscope. Whatever he did, he was punished for it. So he learnt quickly.

One thing the family couldn't stand was the sight of him playing rugby union. When Dad and I would stay up late to watch Stade Francais play on television, we would shake our heads. Mark was just wasted over there, left on the wing and losing half a kilo every week.

He said he matured when he returned from France but, when it comes to his family, we go further than skin deep in how we know each other. I don't judge who he is. I know what he is from being his brother, so I wouldn't say he's changed.

The rest of his brothers and I know him as well as anyone, and we don't judge him like that. He's probably more mature in a football sense and a business sense. I don't judge him from those perspectives.

I reckon he could've kept playing, but he was over it mentally. He'd been playing footy since he was five years old. He never got a break because he played well. But in the end he'd had a gutful of the game behind the scenes. It didn't surprise me when he retired, but I would've liked to have seen him play on. He was well within his rights to say that's enough.

Dean Gasnier, brother
We are a family of four boys, Mark being the youngest, and we share a very close bond as brothers. I was never surprised by what Mark achieved – he was always talented and athletic. He was the type of kid who was good at any sport he attempted and was always extremely competitive. A huge part of Mark's success was Mum and Dad. They were extremely supportive of him throughout his footballing years.

I was proud and nervous for Mark when he made his debut. Over the years he has achieved so much and confronted many injuries, but he seems to come out good at the end of his career. Mark has always been as strong mentally as he is physically.

I will never forget St George winning the Grand Final. It was the icing on the cake for Mark and my family. Going back to the dressing-room for the celebration after the game with Mark, my family and the other players and families is something I will always remember. It was just so well deserved, something that Mark deserved to tick off his list.

Matt Bennett, long-time mate
We went to school together at Peakhurst High, but I lived down the road from him and we grew up together, even though I was a year older.

He would've preferred to be a surfer – that is true. When we finished school, we would take off together and surf. That's all we did growing up: surf and footy. We played together for St George in Harold Matthew Cup, and you could see then that he would go on to achieve what he has. Even before that, coming through the junior ranks for the Dragons, he was our best player – even if he was a year younger than everyone else. He would score all the tries. He was always big. Big for his age. I remember him getting into the pub when he was 13. I don't think he has changed since he was a kid.

I went to Paris and spent some time with him when he was playing rugby union. He tried to be French, he tried to speak the language, but he was nothing like it. When we were over there, he would talk about the possibility of coming back and winning a premiership with the Dragons. That is all he ever wanted to do.

And then he did it.

Paul McGregor, Dragons teammate
I was building my house and some boys rocked up on the Mad Monday and said I had to come for a drink. Gaz stayed

with us that night, and I ended up coming out of retirement and playing footy with him the following season. From that day, we became very good mates.

He had raw talent as a kid, but what impressed me the most was how he carried himself. He had manners, all the tools as a player, and he was respectful. A lot of young players these days carry themselves a little bit higher than what they should. He came from a well-respected family. He didn't want any accolades when he played. He didn't want the raps that go with it. He just wanted to play footy. As a consequence, he became a close friend of my family.

Gaz had many ups and downs during his career, but he did it his way. As soon as he lost the enjoyment out of playing, he didn't want to play anymore. A lot of people with his ability and on his money would've hung around and gone through the motions. He didn't want to be that person. That shows the character within him. There are plenty of players over the years who have held on because they won't earn that kind of money again. He was still at the top of his game and walked away, purely because he had lost the enjoyment of it. For me, that says a lot about the person.

The thing that I admired is his courage to test himself. He went to French rugby because he had to, to a different code in a different country. He came back and tested himself again in rugby league. And then had the spanners to walk away when he could've gone through the motions. Tell me another person in the game who has that toughness.

Peter Doust, St George Illawarra Chief Executive

I had heard about Mark Gasnier long before he knew me. I grew up in the Dragons community and I knew his Uncle Reg very well. Reg was very close to my father, Laurie, who was a long-term official at the club. So I'd always had a soft spot for his family.

Mark came into first grade in 2000, when I'd been in the job of chief executive for a very short period of time, and we struck up a friendship and a professional working relationship very early in the piece. From that point on, we just grew closer and closer.

That was partly because we had some crises during our time. The one I remember most was when he almost went to Wigan at the end of 2004, after he had been sacked from the New South Wales team during Origin. Wigan were so keen, and I was worried about whether we could afford Mark Gasnier in the economic environment.

Gaz always had this out-of-the-box mentality of the world. He always wanted to be out there playing and doing things around the world – he didn't necessarily always want to keep it all at Kogarah, or even with St George Illawarra. It got to the point where I just said to Gaz, 'Mate, I just can't do it to the club and I can't do it to our football team, and so I'm just going to tell you I'm not going to give you a release.' I thought he'd be a bit pissed off about it, but he said, 'I understand.' And then we just moved on. The simple fact of it was we never wanted to see him play for anyone else.

The Origin situation was also tough. I wasn't real happy with the management of the New South Wales Rugby League at the time, because they rang me and just dumped the whole issue on our club. They basically said, 'Well, we've sent him home. He's all yours.' I didn't find that to be very supportive or professional.

We fined Mark but he never challenged it. He never challenged anything that the club did around him over the years, because he had a quality set of values. He might have had his indiscretions from time to time – that day wasn't his best day – but he never had any underlying disrespect for values that had been instilled in him. We all know people who've had aberrations in their growth and development, and if we all had them turn out like Mark Gasnier we wouldn't be too unhappy.

Of course, the other issue we had to deal with was when he left to play French rugby. That was hard on the Dragons – it was not one of our best days – but in saying that it's true that we were not the ones who had let him down financially and commercially. Other people were the cause of his decision to leave.

We were heavily criticised and that was very hard to take. We went on the front foot and we were quite open. We were misrepresented in the more generalised coverage of the subject and more specifically accused of letting him down. I just knew that we, as a club, fulfilled our part of the arrangement, and so did Mark.

When Mark came back, he said he was coming back to do something he hadn't done with us – win a premiership. I remember talking to Wayne Bennett at the time, and the coach had a discussion with the senior players, and they all wanted him back. They were mad keen. It was quite amazing.

The support of his fellow players and the commitment from our football staff to help him prepare, after two years out of the game and no pre-season, was sensational.

In the deed of release, when he went to France, we negotiated that if he did come back and play again in the NRL it had to be with us. There was talk that he might play for Newcastle. That's when I had to remind his management that he couldn't do that. The result was the premiership we had been searching to find for so long. And Mark was a part of it. Unbelievable, isn't it?

People talk about the pressure of playing for the Dragons, or being involved with them as an official. The team Mark was in during the 2005 season, which was probably the best roster we ever put on the field, couldn't do that. Fortunately for Mark, he was part of the premiership in 2010 and he had the chance to contribute and win what he came back to win.

When Mark told me he was retiring the following season, with three seasons to run on his contract, I tried to talk him out of it. Actually, I wanted to make sure he was making the right decision; that he had gone through it thoroughly and he was retiring for the right reasons. We also had to know early, because if he wasn't going to be on our roster in 2012, we needed to make alternative decisions and arrangements.

He had always said he wouldn't let the club down by leaving us in the lurch. And he didn't.

Phil Gould, former NSW Origin coach

I'd been desperate to get him into the Origin side, but through injury and unavailability it had never happened. Then he finally came in for the 2004 series, although he wasn't in the greatest of form at the time. I got the feeling he didn't know if the selectors wanted him there or not. There was a stage of his career when I thought he was the best centre I'd seen. And I believed that.

We had a talk between the two of us. Just about him. I think the constant reference to the name was an annoyance. It seemed to be a source of frustration. I told him I'd always thought he was a great footballer. The advice I gave to him was the same I have given plenty of players over the years. When they're away from football, all they're worrying about is football. When they're at football, they just want to be somewhere else. The footy grind gets them down. They feel they can't do something outside of football because they think it will affect their football. It's constant stress and self-torture. Leave that to the coaches. Just learn to be a footballer when you are at football. Keep yourself in the moment.

That's what I wanted when he came into camp in 2004, before the phone call episode that saw him kicked out. The reason I decided to announce I was quitting Origin two days after he was sacked didn't have anything to do with Gaz. It was more because of the initial investigations, where there had been a few cover-ups. Where I had gone into bat for players but it turned out I'd been lied to. I don't care what players do, if they tell the truth I will stick by them. It wasn't Gaz who lied to me.

I'd thought he was the best centre I'd ever seen for a couple of years before saying it publicly. When I did, people thought, *Oh really?* As I said then, 'Give me someone better.' He was the perfect prototype: fast, elusive, big. He was in control of his game.

Other centres might have been at the top of their game for longer, they might have sustained their run for longer, but there was a period of his career when he was the best I had laid eyes on. He struck fear into those who coached against him. And he was the type of player you wanted in the team. He could 'shimmy-shimmy-*whoosh!*' better than anyone.

It will always be a shame that we didn't see more of him. He was spinning his wheels with injuries there for many years. I was waiting to see this potential blossom into a superstar career. I've seen a lot of great players over the years, and he was one of the ones you wanted to be set free, because they are the players of our era.

I'm glad he realised his potential for some part of his career. He seemed content in himself when he came back from Paris. And it was pleasing for me to hear, after he played Origin in 2011, how good he had been. He had been good with the younger players. A different bloke who enjoyed his footy.

Trent Barrett, Dragons captain and five-eighth

Gaz was one of the best – if not the best – centre I played with. The first time I saw him was when he came into a Dragons pre-season camp in Orange as a 16-year-old in 1999. We all knew he was going to be a great player from the moment we saw him play. He had such unbelievable footwork for such a big man. His agility and his hands and his ability to beat a man one on one was second to none. Gaz was even better on his feet than Paul McGregor, and that is saying something. So powerful, just a natural footballer.

So it was a given that he would achieve what he did in the game. We all knew he would. He was never overawed, he was never nervous. He had everything going for him. But more than that, he was always a humble kid who listened. He never had a big head, and I really enjoyed playing with him. He certainly made me look good on occasions, and I enjoyed having him playing outside of me.

There was a lot of stuff thrown at us during our time at the club. We laughed at most of it – well, we tried to. It was one of the main reasons why I needed a change. It wore me down in the end. I put on a brave face for the boys because I was their captain and leader. And I didn't want them to see that get to me, but in the end it did. I'd had enough, especially after 2005 and 2006 when I thought we had the team to win the competition, and when I joined Wigan it was like a big weight lifted off my shoulders.

When I left, Gaz felt the criticism much more because he suddenly became the highest profile player at the club. Jason Ryles copped the blowtorch, too. It comes with the territory, but at that club there seemed to be much more.

When the Dragons won the premiership in 2010, I was really happy for Gaz – for all of them. They were mates that I had played plenty of footy with, and I'd seen a lot of them come through the SG Ball and Jersey Flegg ranks and then into first grade. I would like to think that along the way I have helped one of them at some stage, and I got a kick out of that. I won't lie: there were parts of me that made me wish I was there with them for that Grand Final day. Or if we had done it in 2005 or 2006. That will never go away.

But I was happy that it worked out for Gaz the way it did, because he deserved it.

Ricky Stuart, former Kangaroos and NSW coach

Gaz might think I was angry with him when he went to French rugby, but it was never personal. I just felt there were too many people running off to the other code for the money. I had a firm belief then that those who defected to rugby should be banned from returning for two years. That was my issue with the people who ran the game – not a personal one with Mark.

He was always a stylish, attacking footballer. Beautiful agility and speed. He could really hold a player up and make them look silly, but he could also do that with his hands. Mark's a very intelligent footballer. During the 2011 Origin series, he was very helpful in getting the right edge structured in defence for New South Wales. He was positive and knew what he wanted in attack, because that's what experienced senior players do. It was a significant big jump from 2005, when I first had him in the Blues side.

I'd wanted him for that Origin series, despite what had happened the year before. He was the best centre, for a start. And everyone makes mistakes in life. He comes from a good family and he's a decent bloke. He turned into a leader for young blokes around him.

The thing I noticed about Gaz was how he matured. He was a young bloke who enjoyed a good time out. He was the life of the party. A lot of us have been over the years. But he made a decision to stop doing that at the right time of his career, and it gave him the longevity that it did.

There are certain players you coach at rep level, and you get a greater feel for them more than others. After that 2005 series, and then during our time together with the Kangaroos, I came to see him as a mate. When I saw that tackle from Steve Matai, I came in support of him for that reason. The tackle was cheap. He had eliminated one of the best players in the game and it could've done some real damage. You defend people you know and trust. Mark had done so much for me in representative football. It was my responsibility to defend him.

Jason Nightingale, Dragons teammate
We both come from the same junior club, Renown United, but I didn't get to know him until I played in the under-20s. Because I was a St George junior, he went out of his way to introduce himself. When I did make first grade, I had the pleasure of playing outside of him on the right wing.

Gaz was everything you wanted in a right centre. He could create something out of nothing, just with pure speed, power and footwork. As a winger, you can't ask for much more than that from your centre.

He backed himself. He knew if he put himself in the position where he was one on one with his opposite player, he knew he could beat him. That attracted defenders to him. That's why a lot of wingers benefitted from playing outside of him. Because of the aura he carried, he attracted more than one defender, because defences knew if you didn't he was inevitably going to beat them.

He would beat them with his step, which some people called the 'shimmy-shimmy-*whoosh!*' It wasn't much off that: a lot of stutter, a lot of short movements, and then he could go either way. A little bit subtle then . . . BOOM!

Gaz might say differently, but he embraced the 'shimmy-shimmy-*whoosh!*' I noticed it was written on his boots one day. He wore them for two years. I've got a pair of his boots at my place now that just says 'Gasnier' on them. But he did have the 'shimmy-shimmy-*whoosh!*' boots.

His stand-out games were the ones I wasn't involved in. That Wests Tigers games, when he scored four tries, stands above the rest. I was playing lower grades at the time, and that was the best all-round individual performance you will ever see from a centre.

Because we would drive from Sydney to Wollongong for training and back, I reckon we've done over 20,000 kilometres in the car together. Just before he went to France, he was living in Manly, so he was doing 50 kilometres before he got to me in Blakehurst.

It was a hard time when he was having contract problems in 2008. He spoke to me a little bit about it, but not in great depth. He didn't really open up to me about it until he did the deal. 'I need to do this for me,' he said. I completely understood: he wasn't getting what he was promised. There were other stresses, too, that were coming externally. He needed a break. The pressure that comes with signing a big deal like the one he did with the Dragons in the first place was huge. That all built up.

Going to Paris allowed him to get away from the fishbowl of rugby league in Australia. That is something he would say has defined his life and he wouldn't regret that for a second. Everyone at the club knew why he made his decision.

When he announced his retirement, I wasn't surprised. I could see it coming. He said it quite often on those trips home that it would be his last year. But I didn't believe him because I could see how hungry he was when he was actually doing it. I thought he was gee-ing up. He obviously wasn't. The game was wearing him down, trying to find the motivation all the time. He's competitive enough to know that if he's not 100 per cent committed mentally he shouldn't be doing it.

Everyone who knows Gaz knows why he did it, and why he retired. You look at him now and see all the opportunities he's taken – it justifies his decision to leave.

Andrew Gray, Performance Director, St George Illawarra Dragons

I've been with the Dragons since the merger in 1999, and I was physiotherapist and rehabilitation coordinator back then. I can remember Gaz playing junior reps. He always had unbelievable acceleration and an ability to change direction at speed. After evading an opponent he could get going again in a couple of steps. The way he changed direction so late towards the line, without any regard for his own safety, had a fair bit to do with him being as brilliant as he was, but it surely contributed to so many of his contact injuries. He would train the same way.

Gaz had an ability to get a lot of little muscle strains during training, keeping medical staff very busy. At times these injuries prevent players from training and playing, but he would play on. Looking back, we took a lot of risks with Gaz playing with injury. Not many players have that in them.

Gaz spent several extended periods of time in rehabilitation from contact injuries. Whenever he was sidelined for an extended period of time with injury, he was very resilient and positive. He became experienced with his rehab. He got better as he got older and was exceptional in this regard when he returned from Paris. Dealing with the disappointment of injury and training with pain, going through the rehab process and being positive on the days when you really don't feel like it, is something the best players learn. Some guys can do it, some can't. Gaz became better as his career went on.

The pectoral injury was his worst and came at the worst possible time. Those injuries have a real characteristic feel to them. The player feels a 'pop', and with a quick muscle test on the field you know straightaway. I could feel the tendon was ruptured away from the bone. Once they're gone, they're gone.

That was devastating for the whole club. He was our five-eighth at the time, a new position for him, and he'd had a fantastic pre-season. That had a flow-on effect for the rest of season and we missed the finals. He came back early from that injury. I had to hold him back. He wanted to return two weeks earlier than he did. The way he rehabilitated that injury was outstanding.

His deep pelvic muscle tear was a very rare injury. There aren't many reported cases. Once again, it was from putting such a large amount of force into the ground to push his body sideways. Sometimes he stepped so hard that he went beyond what his body could handle. It was a good one.

I'd had a long relationship with Gaz, so when he returned from Paris we started on his comeback to the NRL, training in secret to reduce the media interest around him being back in the country. We did a lot of work, just the two of us. They were some tough times then because the amount of work you do in French rugby, as a winger, compared to what an NRL centre does is significantly different. Gaz was coming from a low base at the time. We basically had to rebuild and start again.

He was only ever two or three kilos underweight at that time. He had a higher body fat level but lower muscle bulk. His weight wasn't that different. The athletes with the best genetic make-up get it back quickly, and he did. There isn't much protein in camembert cheese and baguettes.

The Grand Final victory made so many people at our club happy. It was so good that Gaz had come back for the right reasons, and finally got the premiership he deserved. I wasn't surprised when he retired, but I was disappointed because I firmly believed he had two seasons left.

People might ask what might have been if he hadn't suffered so many injuries, but I think he had a fantastic career. He made a decision as a youngster that he was going to do things 'flat-out'. When you do that, you often get hurt. He could've toned down the way he was playing, but he wouldn't have been the Mark Gasnier that everyone will remember.

Wayne Bennett, former Dragons coach

All the players there certainly wanted him back. They'd told me how much he'd matured, and how much the Dragons meant to him. They all knew him better than I'll ever know him, and they had a lot of respect for him. The key part was that he lived in Cronulla, not Manly, like he did before he left for France, so it wasn't a long drive to Wollongong for training. The second thing was who would be paying the bills and who wouldn't if he came back. He was terribly distracted with his contract when he left in 2008, and I didn't want that happening a second time around.

There was a lot of talk when he came back about him disrupting the balance of the team. That never happened. He was a plus from day one. After a couple of weeks, he wanted to talk tactics. He said, 'I'm too busy defending.' I said, 'That's a fair call, mate.' I knew he could tackle but I wanted to make sure his defence was right, so I threw him in the deep end and he did a great job for us.

The Mark Gasnier of yesteryear made all the breaks. But when he came back, the superstar wasn't just a player anymore. He was a different player. A much more mature player. A very team-orientated and very defence-orientated player. In the Grand Final, he came up with a couple of plays that nobody else could.

The Dragons are such an important part of the game's history. It's something you've got to be careful about when you are a part of it, because it can consume you. They'd been 31 years without a premiership. People looked up to these men to deliver that year. The club's rich, rich history had created a lot of pressure.

When it happened, it meant a lot to so many people. But it meant more to the players who had given their lives to the club: Ben Hornby, Ben Creagh, Matt Cooper, Dean Young . . . and Gaz.

It was the absolute crowning of all their achievements. It will be the one that they will treasure the most.

Ben Hornby, Dragons captain

I played against him in Harold Matthews when I was representing Illawarra, and he was playing for St George, and we all knew of this boom young kid who everyone was talking about. After that, I played some Premier League alongside him for the Dragons, and we came into first grade in the same year. In those early seasons, it was pretty simple: if Gaz made a break, it was a try. Big, strong, fast – if he got through the line it was all over. He had the rare gift of speed and strength.

When he told us that he was leaving to play rugby in Paris, it came about so fast. He said he wanted to do something else, and a month later we were knocked out and he was gone. It was tough because it had happened so suddenly. It was a big loss for us.

I always felt he would come back. I'd kept in touch while he was over in Paris and, while he was saying that he was enjoying it over there, I always got the feeling he was going to make a return.

For the first few weeks, he would have admitted that he wasn't playing his best, but he brought that class to our backline and he could still find the tryline. It was said that his return destabilised a winning team. I'm not sure if it rattled anyone, but we had to fit him into the side – an established side that was winning. There was a lot of pressure on him to come back in and be the Mark Gasnier that he was before. We were as a side going well, so it was a no-win situation for Gaz. We always had faith that he was going to come good and become the Gaz he was before. It wasn't going to happen straightaway, but we persisted and the rewards came later on. The premiership could not have been any better.

Was I surprised when he retired? A little bit. Gaz had spoken about it, but I did't know how serious he was. I just thought at 29 he had more years left in him.

Jason Ryles, former Dragons teammate and best man
He has the biggest chin in the game, although we are in the final together. But that's not where the similarities start and finish.

Gaz and I have been good mates for a long time, because we are the same age and we came through at the Dragons at the same time. There was a lot of expectation on the Dragons in those days. That said, I understand any Dragons team is always going to have massive expectations. It goes with the territory of that club.

But the strength of the roster we had during our time together at the club meant the scrutiny and the interest was pretty intense. That in itself brought Gaz and me closer together, for sure. But we had a good time. We were young and went out together, and that drew a lot of us closer.

The best part about playing with Gaz is that when the game was tight, when he was on, he always found a way to find the play that would win it for us, especially in 2004 through to 2006 when he was in the best form of his career. He had that ability to pull us out of the shit whenever we were in it. I couldn't tell you the amount of games we won because of him.

For that reason, the 2010 Grand Final was always going to be strange for both of us. It was an unbelievable circumstance: I was playing against the side that I had played most of my footy for, and I wanted nothing more than to beat them. It was bizarre. I hardly spoke to Gaz early in the week, but that was it. When it was over, he was one of the first people to come to me and shake my hand. The feeling I had wasn't too good. It was an emotional time. But a small part of me was happy about it, for him.

MARK GASNIER STATISTICS

CAREER OVERVIEW

	Games	Trs	Gls	F/G	Pts
CLUB CAREER 2000–11					
St George Illawarra 2000–11					
Premiership Games *2000–11*	174	92	26	-	420
World Club Challenge *2011*	1	-	-	-	0
TOTAL	**175**	**92**	**26**	**-**	**420**
REPRESENTATIVE CAREER 2001, 2003–08, 2011					
CITY–COUNTRY 2001, 2003					
City Origin *2001, 2003*	2	1	-	-	4
STATE OF ORIGIN 2004–06, 2008, 2011					
New South Wales *2004–06, 2008, 2011*	12	4	1	-	18
AUSTRALIA 2001, 2005–08					
Tests *2001, 2005–08*	15	11	-	-	44
OTHER REPRESENTATIVE 2007					
Australian Prime Minister's XIII *2007*	1	-	-	-	0
GRAND TOTAL					
All senior matches	**205**	**108**	**27**	**-**	**486**

	Games	Tries	Goals	F/Goals	Points	P	W	L	D	Position
2000	8	5	-	-	20	26	12	14	-	9th
2001	28	11	-	-	44	28	13	13	2	Semifinalists
2002	14	12	3	-	54	26	10	13	2	Semifinalists
2003	13	8	-	-	32	24	11	13	-	10th
2004	12	11	-	-	44	25	14	11	-	Quarterfinalists
2005	19	8	4	-	40	26	17	9	-	Prelim. finalists
2006	23	18	1	-	74	27	16	11	-	Prelim. finalists
2007	6	2	-	-	8	24	9	15	-	13th
2008	18	6	18	-	60	25	13	12	-	Quarterfinalists
2010	12	5	-	-	20	27	20	7	-	Premiers
2011	21	6	-	-	24	26	14	11	1	Semifinalists
TOTAL	174	92	26	-	420					

Junior Football: Renown United

Australian Schoolboys: 1998, 1999 (from Peakhurst High School)

Junior Representative: NSW Under-17s 1998, NSW Under-19s 1999

Premiership debut: St George Illawarra v Newcastle at Marathon Stadium, 24/3/2000 (Rd 8)

Premierships: 2010

Finals series: 2001, 2002, 2004, 2005, 2006, 2008, 2010, 2011

Captaincy: 22 games (2007–08); 11 wins, 11 losses

Coaches: David Waite (2000), Andrew Farrar (2000–02), Nathan Brown (2003-08), Wayne Bennett (2010–11)

Awards:
Dally M Centre of the Year: 2005, 2006
St George Illawarra Player of the Year: 2006 (joint-winner)

STATE OF ORIGIN 2004–2011

No.	Date	Venue	Game	Tries	Goals	F/G	Points	Result	Score
1	07/07/2004	Telstra Stadium	3	2	1	-	10	Won	36–14
2	25/05/2005	Suncorp Stadium	1	1	-	-	4	Lost	20–24
3	22/06/2005	Telstra Stadium	2	-	-	-	-	Won	32–22
4	06/07/2005	Suncorp Stadium	3	1	-	-	4	Won	32–10
5	24/05/2006	Telstra Stadium	1	-	-	-	-	Won	17–16
6	14/06/2006	Suncorp Stadium	2	-	-	-	-	Lost	6–30
7	05/07/2006	Telstra Dome	3	-	-	-	-	Lost	14–16
8	21/05/2008	ANZ Stadium, Sydney	1	-	-	-	-	Won	18–10
9	11/06/2008	Suncorp Stadium	2	-	-	-	-	Lost	0–30
10	25/05/2011	Suncorp Stadium	1	-	-	-	-	Lost	12–16
11	15/06/2011	ANZ Stadium, Sydney	2	-	-	-	-	Won	18–8
12	06/07/2011	Suncorp Stadium	3	-	-	-	-	Lost	24–34

Notes on venues: Telstra Stadium and ANZ Stadium, Sydney, refer to Sydney's Olympic Stadium at Homebush. Telstra Dome refers to Melbourne's Docklands Stadium (now known as Etihad Stadium).

Position: Played centre in all matches except Game 3, 2006 when he was five-eighth.

Coaches: Phil Gould 2004, Ricky Stuart 2005, 2011, Graham Murray 2006–07, Craig Bellamy 2008.

Summary of matches: 12 games, four tries, one goal, 18 points. Won six, lost six.

TEST CAREER 2001–2008

No.	Date	Opponent	Venue	Status	T	G	FG	Pts	Result	Score
1	07/10/2001	Papua New Guinea	Lloyd Robson Oval, Port Moresby	Test	1	-	-	4	Won	54-12
2	15/10/2005	New Zealand	Telstra Stadium, Sydney	Tri-N	2	-	-	8	Lost	28-38
3	21/10/2005	New Zealand	Ericsson Stadium, Auckland	Tri-N	1	-	-	4	Won	28-26
4	05/11/2005	Great Britain	JJB Stadium, Wigan	Tri-N	-	-	-	0	Won	20-6
5	12/11/2005	France	Stade Aime Giral Perpignan	Tri-N	-	-	-	0	Won	44-12
6	19/11/2005	Great Britain	KC Stadium, Hull	Tri-N	1	-	-	4	Won	26-14
7	26/11/2005	New Zealand	Elland Road, Leeds	Tri-N Final	-	-	-	0	Lost	0-24
8	05/05/2006	New Zealand	Suncorp Stadium, Brisbane	Test	1	-	-	4	Won	50-12
9	14/10/2006	New Zealand	Mt Smart Stadium, Auckland	Tri-N	1	-	-	4	Won	30-18
10	21/10/2006	New Zealand	Telstra Dome, Melbourne	Tri-N	1	-	-	4	Won	20-15
11	04/11/2006	Great Britain	Aussie Stadium, Sydney	Tri-N	-	-	-	0	Lost	12-23
12	18/11/2006	Great Britain	Suncorp Stadium, Brisbane	Tri-N	1	-	-	4	Won	33-10
13	25/11/2006	New Zealand	Aussie Stadium, Sydney	Tri-N Final	-	-	-	0	Won	16-12
14	14/10/2007	New Zealand	Westpac Stadium, Wellington	Tri-N	-	-	-	0	Won	58-0
15	09/05/2008	New Zealand	Sydney Cricket Ground	Test	2	-	-	8	Won	28-12

Notes on venues: Telstra Stadium and ANZ Stadium, Sydney refer to Sydney's Olympic Stadium at Homebush. Telstra Dome refers to Melbourne's Docklands Stadium (now known as Etihad Stadium). Mt Smart Stadium, Auckland was formerly known as Ericsson Stadium. Aussie Stadium refers to Sydney Football Stadium (now known as Allianz Stadium).

Status key: Tri N = Tri Nations

Position: Centre in all Test matches

Coaches: Chris Anderson 2001, Wayne Bennett 2005, Ricky Stuart 2006–08

Summary of matches: 15 Tests, 11 tries, 44 points. Won 12, lost three.

Statistics by David Middleton, League Information Services, 2012

ACKNOWLEDGEMENTS

Writing this book has been an amazing experience, and not just because I was able to tell the truth about my career and everything that surrounds it. I had the opportunity to listen to my family and closest friends open up about me in ways they might not always do face to face. These words are even more important because they are the people who have defined me as a person and, ultimately, the people who I didn't want to let down throughout my life and career. So, to all those people I have mentioned throughout the book and every player, ex-player and guy grew up with, I thank you so much for your support and friendship. I must make special mention of my family: Mum, Dad, Gavin, Brent and Dean. You guys are responsible for everything I have achieved in life – and not just on the football field. I love you guys to death. Thank you so much!

To Random House, my publishers, you have been a pleasure to work with and I thank you so much for your support and help throughout this experience. Andrew Webster, you have been unreal, mate. We definitely kept the coffee shops in business – and I even know how to type now! – but, above that, your amazing ability and writing experience have given me the opportunity to portray my story as best as I possibly can. Thank you.

I saved this person for last on purpose: my wife, Claudine. I won't get too lovey-dovey, but I will say that I have all the love and respect for you in the world. We have been through so much together in a short span of time, and it's only bought us closer together. You are an amazing person and, above all, a wonderful mother. And thanks to Kalani for deleting lots and ripping out the power cord as much as possible!

M. G.

A big thanks to everyone at Random House, especially Brandon VanOver for his professionalism and patience. Also to Mark's friends, family and past and present team-mates for making themselves available for interviews. And, of course, to Gaz, for letting me push him into areas he might not have wanted to go. Go Dragons!

A. W.

ANDREW WEBSTER is the Chief League Writer for *The Daily Telegraph*. This is his second book following *Supercoach: The Life and Times of Jack Gibson*.